DARTMOOR'S
WAR PRISON & CHURCH
1805 - 1817

Elisabeth Stanbrook

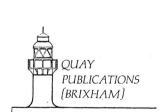

QUAY
PUBLICATIONS
(BRIXHAM)

Quay Publications (Brixham)
Tavistock

First published in Great Britain in 2002 by
Quay Publications (Brixham),
P.O. Box 16,
Tavistock,
Devon
PL19 0XR
www.dartmoormagazine.co.uk

ISBN 1 870083 45 8

British Library Cataloguing in Publication Data
A catalogue record of this title is available from the British Library

Designed and printed by Kingfisher Print & Design Ltd, Totnes, Devon TQ9 5XN

Front cover: A watercolour sketch of Dartmoor Prison in 1813 by Captain Durrant, one of the
militia on duty at the time. *Hampshire County Council Museums Service.*

Back cover: Prison No.4 under construction in June 1807, drawn by Samuel Prout.
Collection: Plymouth City Museum & Art Gallery.

CONTENTS

LIST OF ILLUSTRATIONS

INTRODUCTION

'on top of a mountain those prisons does stand
A place pich[t] on purpose for tormenting man
Where Frenchmen and Yankey's together must stay
Until the War's o'er or else run away'

Joseph Velpey 1815

Thomas Tyrwhitt.
Courtesy Christ Church.

Dartmoor Prison at Princetown was built, not only against the backdrop of war but also against a fervent enclosure movement and a desire to make money from large acreages of uncultivated land. The building of this huge complex was a departure from agriculture, but it helped to offset the failure of one man to farm high Dartmoor's land with crops on the scale he had envisaged.

The roots of the late 18th century and early 19th century enclosure movement grew out of various factors; the importance of owning land for political reasons, a growth in the population due to improving living conditions, and a decline in home produced food as people migrated to cities and towns for employment.

On Dartmoor, vast acres of land were being enclosed including Duchy of Cornwall land around what was to become Princetown. Judge Francis Buller was leasing land at Prince Hall (bought from Mr Gullet), as was Tavistock solicitor Mr Edward Bray at Beardown Farm. Mr (later Sir) Thomas Tyrwhitt enclosed 2,300 acres of land to the south west of Two Bridges and built his Tor Royal estate which included a few houses in Princetown (originally Prince(s) Town after his friend the Prince Regent). Tyrwhitt's intention, as with the other enclosers, was to develop a large agricultural estate but, despite small successes in the beginning, with corn, flax (for which he received a medal from the Bath Agricultural Society) and root crops,

Tor Royal, built for Thomas Tyrwhitt.
Valentine.

the venture failed as intended crops could not survive the climate and soil Dartmoor provided.

Tyrwhitt, Private Secretary and good friend of the Prince Regent, was a powerful man. He held many prestigious posts including Auditor and Secretary to the Duchy of Cornwall and Keeper of the Privy Seal (1796-1803), Lord Warden of the Stannaries (1803-12), Vice Admiral of Devon and Cornwall (1805), Gentleman Usher of the Black Rod (1812-32) and also enjoyed time as a Member of Parliament for both Okehampton and Plymouth. Thus he was in a good position to exert his influence and promote the building of a new war prison next to his Dartmoor estate. Prisoners of war came under the auspices of the Admiralty's Transport Office.

Unknown to Tyrwhitt at the time of taking his lease in 1785, the events that were to shape the future of Princetown were only a few years away. In 1799, Napoleon Bonaparte had overthrown the ruling Directory and made himself dictator. From 1804 to early 1814 and in 1815, he was Emperor of the French. From 1803, when he broke the peace treaty of Amiens, he attempted to conquer Europe and met fierce opposition from Britain. As a consequence, many French prisoners were taken and housed in prisons such as those of Norman Cross near Peterborough and Stapleton near Bristol. When these became full, prisoners were held in hulks in the Hamoaze off Plymouth Sound in appalling conditions. Napoleon abdicated in April 1814 and was sent to the island of Elba, but he escaped in March 1815 and regained power for 100 days. He was eventually defeated at the Battle of Waterloo and was exiled on the island of St Helena where he died in 1821.

The American War of 1812 brought another influx of prisoners to British soil. Congress had declared war on Britain on 18 June, objecting to her insistence in searching American vessels for deserters in her battle against Napoleon and for press ganging their crews into service against the French. They also objected to the British giving the Indians in Upper Canada guns and ammunition to thwart American advances in favour of their own stronghold there. The first American prisoners started arriving in Britain in 1813 and some were sent to Dartmoor Prison.

It was the condition of the French prisoners aboard the rotting hulks in the Hamoaze that gave rise to Dartmoor Prison, originally named 'The Depot at Dartmoor'. Tyrwhitt, not one to miss an opportunity, and realising his lack of success at large scale crop growing, advocated putting nearby Duchy of Cornwall land to this other use - he probably foresaw the usefulness of prisoners as labourers too!

One can only wonder at the sheer scale and impact the whole complex, housing thousands of people, had on this remote part of Devon. It was not attached to an urban settlement but stood isolated in all its grimness, requiring constant supplies and maintenance. Two prisoners of war, Frenchman Louis Catel, and American Charles Andrews, gave their independent reactions to their first sight of Dartmoor Prison; both have remarkable similarities:

'... under a dark and gloomy sky, in a cold and foggy climate, on hilly ground, barren, practically denuded, covered for eight months of the year by a mantle of snow, is a surrounding expanse of several square leagues [miles]'.[1]

'... is surrounded on all sides, as far as the eye can see, by the gloomy features of a black moor, uncultivated and uninhabited except by one or two miserable cottages... The place is deprived of everything that is pleasant or agreeable'.[2]

Many books have been written about Dartmoor Prison, with chapters on its initial phase as a prison of war. One of the most detailed is *The Story of Dartmoor Prison* by Basil Thomson, one-time Governor, whose history, which includes the convict prison, was published in 1907. Most authors, understandably, have relied heavily upon his account and also that of Charles Andrew.

The aim of this book is not to concentrate merely on the often repeated stories about the endless escapes, hardships, misdemeanours, murders and suicides. Instead, it gives a chronological insight into the actual building of the prison, including the church, and the many and varied problems associated with running and staffing such a large institution.

By the time the prison of war had closed in 1816, the complex included seven Prison blocks, the Cachot (a punishment cell), four airing sheds, an H-shaped Hospital and a U-shaped Petty Officers' Prison (the latter both 3 storeys high), and the Agent's and surgeon's houses with associated offices and outbuildings. Behind the surgeon's house to the north west of the complex were carpenters' shops and stores, turnkeys' accommodation and the prisoners' shoe shed. Behind the Agent's house to the south west was a porter's lodge, accommodation for stewards, Hospital clerks and turnkeys. Across the western section of the Military Way and in front of the Hospital was a drying house, wash houses, laundry, accommodation for the matron, the surgeon's four rooms, a dispensary and another porter's lodge. A polygonal store stood on the north side of the entrance to the market square and on the south side a matching polygonal building was divided into stores and prisons for wayward militia, a blacksmith and a coopers shop. The other buildings included a receiving house, guard houses, sentry boxes, privies, ash pits, an inner boundary wall comprising iron railings and two granite perimeter walls. There were various associated buildings outside the prison including the dead house (mortuary), the straw house, the reservoir, the Barracks and, of course, the Church and Parsonage House nearby which are given a separate chapter in this book.

The suffering of French and American prisoners of war, so far from home, was very real and desperately sad. Boredom and misery often led to serious incidents that could, as mentioned above, culminate in murder or suicide. Illness was rife and food quality various. These were factors which the Transport Board had to cope with on top of maintaining and running a huge enterprise.

While researching, I found numerous references to names of people living in the area and employed at the prison; some of these families are still with us today. I have included an Appendix of these names and hope that it may prove useful to those interested in local family histories.

Elisabeth Stanbrook
September 2002

1805 - 1807
'Great hindrance and delay'

On 26 June 1805 the Board of the Transport Office 'submitted the propriety of erecting a Prison on Dartmoor capable of containing 5,000 Prisoners, and proposed that one of their Commissioners of this Board with a Surveyor should proceed to Dartmoor for the Purpose of selecting a situation for the intended Buildings that a Plan & Estimate should be forthwith procured'[3] Two days later this was approved, and an architect was sought.

This architect was Mr Daniel Asher Alexander who had trained at the Royal Academy. His address was given as Cattistock, Dorchester, Dorset. He received instructions for an initial meeting with the Admiralty 'at Mr Tyrwhitt's at Tor Royal' on 18 July, where he would meet Commissioner Bouverie. His radial design of the War Prison which, in his own words, afforded 'complete separation and ventilation to the whole',[4] is thought to have been based on William Blackburn's 1785 design of Liverpool Borough Gaol.[5] In all, Alexander was to make twenty-two separate journeys to Dartmoor during the prison's construction.

In the meantime, on 15 July, *The Bristol Times & Mirror* reported that 'Mr Tyrwhitt has suggested to Government the propriety of erecting a building near the above [Princetown] for depositing such prisoners of war as shall be brought into Plymouth; who can, without difficulty, be conveyed up the river Tamar, and landed a few miles from the spot. It is said that this plan will be acted upon forthwith, and barracks built for the reception of a proportionate number of troops'. The landing place in question was Lopwell Quay.

In late September Mr Alexander's first estimate for the works was £86,423 13s 4d, the prison to hold 5,282 men. This could be increased by £17,901 3s 4d (to over £104,000) if 8,370 men were accommodated. This rather exceeded the Admiralty's expectations and they felt the government would balk at this amount. He was compelled to submit another estimate, reducing the acreage for the actual prison complex from 23 to 15 acres and 2 roods, (although he later claimed it was 22 acres)[6] which was £70,146 4s 10d. About three quarters of this amount was for meeting labour costs. The total acreage for the War Depot was 390 acres, on land owned by the Duchy of Cornwall. They sent a communication via Tyrwhitt stating that a 99-year lease on this 'would be the proper step in the first instance previously to the final alienation by Act of Parliament from the Dutchy [sic] to the Crown'.[7] In fact, this Act did not happen and the lease was held by the Admiralty until 1816 when the prison was vacated.

The plot of land chosen, certainly by the Admiralty and the architect, was near Tyrwhitt's lodges. A later account claims this place was chosen because 'the water is excellent and plentiful (which is true of most parts of the moor); the soil is gravel (which it is not); that the site is covered with peat from two to four feet deep, which will be useful for fuel; that there is building stone upon the spot; and lastly - the only sound reason - that it is near the turnpike road frequented by carriers from Moreton [sic] and Ashburton, who would be content to sell their wares at a cheaper rate instead of carrying them on to Plymouth'.[8] Alexander himself said that the abundance of peat 'was the leading idea of fixing the prison on that spot'.[9] However, it would seem that Tyrwhitt also favoured the site as it was more in keeping with his original plans for a settlement here. The foundations of what is locally reputed to be a Napoleonic look-out, known as the Castle, can be found in the southernmost enclosure south of South Hessary House near Peat Cot, although the records did not refer to it.

Once the Depot site was chosen, the builders had to be found. On 18 October 1805, the Transport Office issued a notice which appeared in the *Exeter Flying Post* on 24 October. It invited tenders for the building of a War Prison for 5,000 prisoners, to be received by them on 16 December. Plans and specifications were available for perusal on Monday 18 November at both the Transport Office and at Tor Royal. The prison was 'to be constructed of moor stone to be broken from the scattered rocks on the spot, where there is also fine gravel, sand and water; they are to be floored with timber, and roofed with timber and slate'.

The area within the prison boundary was always known as 'Dartmoor' while the area falling outside was usually called Prince(s) Town.

The track from Tavistock to Moretonhampstead became a turnpike road in 1772 while that between Roborough Rock and Two Bridges had to wait another 40 years. This 1812 road had a branch opposite the Plume of Feathers which went past the Depot and linked up with the road from Tavistock. Before 1812, the ancient track from Roborough Rock on which Tyrwhitt as the founder of Tor Royal, and the suppliers to the prison from the Plymouth area, had to travel, was in very poor condition due to wear and tear which must have contributed to the road being turnpiked. The Act of Parliament dated 28 February 1812 stated that it was much out of repair 'and in many Places narrow and ineffectually mended, widened, turned, altered, improved and kept in good Repair by the ordinary Course of law'.[10] Many familiar names are listed as trustees including Daniel Alexander, Edward Bray, Isaac Cotgrave, Sir Massey Lopes, Revd James Holman Mason and Joshua Rowe. Although not mentioned in the Act, ready labour from the prisoners for the road in the vicinity of the Depot was to prove most convenient as contemporary records show.

Although contracts for the building work had not been finalised, towards the end of 1805 workmen were employed preparing the site. The weather, notorious in and around Princetown, was affecting progress with wagon wheels badly rutting the rough roads in the vicinity. 'This hath been a hindering week... the sun hath scarcely made its appearance and we may safely say that £120 hath been lost this way in wages'.[11]

By January 1806 the lowest proposal, out of four from Plymouth firms received by the Admiralty for building the prison, was £66,800 which was £3,346 14s 6d less than Alexander's second estimate. This firm was Messrs Isbell, Hartland, Rowe & Holland (usually referred to as Messrs Isbell & Co) and their tender was successful. In addition, they wanted to be sole distributors of spirits and beer to the workmen employed by them. This request was granted by the Admiralty and was hopefully a more lucrative contract than that for building the prison! Their remuneration for the building work was paid to them in instalments - usually between £2,000 and £3,600 at a time.

The main buildings in the prison complex itself were to comprise:

5 Prison buildings to house 1000 men each (costing c. £5,107 each)

A Hospital (costing £7,951 5s 1d)

Petty Officers' Prison (costing £3,107 7s 11d)

Barracks for 500 troops (costing £5,004 7s)

Boundary walls and water courses were to cost £14,489 13s 1d.

Quantities of moor stone were used for building work but it was on such a large scale that a quarry, to become known as Herne Hole Quarry, was opened just a few hundred yards to the northwest. From here, tramlines (or an iron railway) were laid to the building site.

Initially, the workforce employed on the building of the Depot was to be from the Regiment of Devon Militia. This was objected to by their Commander-in-Chief so consideration was given to bringing down masons from the Yorkshire Moors. In the end, labour came from Cornwall as the Cornish masons were cheaper to employ - at first!

On 20 March 1806 Thomas Tyrwhitt laid the foundation stone. It is unfortunate that this appears to have been lost.

The War, the whole reason for the building of the Depot, impeded progress on several occasions. The initial price given for the building work had not really taken into consideration increases in costs. In April 1806, Messrs Isbell & Co were demanding an extra allowance for timber due to rising costs from £5 to £7 a consignment. This was caused by 'the shutting of the Sound & that a clause might be inserted in the contract [which they had not signed yet] to allow them additional Duty which might be laid on timber & iron'.[12] The Admiralty were not sympathetic and refused amendments to the contract, but they did concede to pay an allowance for any additional duty if imposed.

The Cornish masons then demanded higher pay and, as a consequence, labour costs rose by one

Two stone-trolleys plus wheelbarrows used in the construction of Dartmoor Prison, as sketched by Samuel Prout on 21 October 1806.
Collection: Plymouth City Museum & Art Gallery.

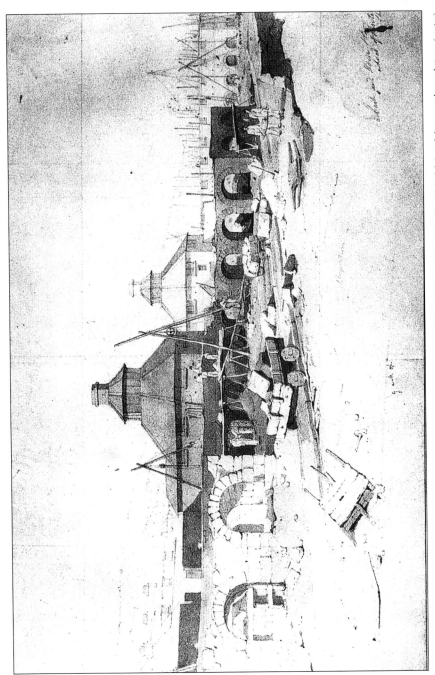

A pencil and wash sketch made on 1 June 1807 by Samuel Prout of the arches of the Petty Officers' Prison (left) and the Hospital (right), and the two polygonal stores (centre). *Collection: Plymouth City Museum & Art Gallery.*

From west to east, showing the five Prison blocks under construction. On the extreme left is the Hospital, while on the right is one of the polygonal stores. A pencil and wash sketch by Samuel Prout on 2 June 1807.
Collection: Plymouth City Museum & Art Gallery.

fifth. Also, the price of timber continued to increase, and by December 1806, it had risen to £8 8s per load. But the Admiralty still refused to pay the difference. As a result, the masons threatened to walk out leaving the prison unfinished. The Admiralty, seeing the finishing date being pushed back and back, gave way and supplied timber from the Devonport dockyard; as a consequence, many of the prison beams installed were timbers from ships.

Mr William Bough was given a contract for removing peat from the moor and was paid £200 in the first instance.

Messrs Isbell & Co's contract was not signed until June 1806, by which time one of their sureties had been dead for 5 months without a replacement having been found. Despite this, they expressed confidence that their contractual obligations would be fulfilled within a year. Their letter to the Admiralty reveals the work undertaken so far: 'boundary walls at Dartmoor half built, the Turnkey Houses were built, the Airing Sheds ready to put up, the Cookhouse about one third built, and that nothing but bad weather could prevent the Contract being completed in the next year'.[13] This proved a rather naive hope!

By the end of November, Mr Alexander was asked by the Admiralty to propose a plan for accommodation of a surgeon, a dispenser and two assistant surgeons. They also instructed him to continue with the pallisading at the sides of the Petty Officers' Prison (known as 'Le Petit Cautionnement' by the French) and also those on the Hospital side.

Concern for the welfare of the workforce did not seem a high priority. In December, the Admiralty told Mr Alexander that the government could not pay for providing medical assistance for the contractor's workmen. However, if they paid 4s a day collectively to a Naval surgeon, the Board would appoint one on half pay to reside at Dartmoor. It would seem that the workmen approved this scheme because, from early 1807, they contributed to a fund which reached the required sum to get their surgeon.

By March 1807 the surgeon, Mr Lane, had been employed. He was obviously feeling the cold so characteristic of Princetown as he tried ordering some coal and candles. But this request was refused. His dispensing equipment order, including items to deal with fractures, met no resistance and this was fulfilled from Plymouth. In October 1807, Dr George Magrath offered his services as surgeon to the new Depot, and he was told that although it would not be ready for several months, the Board would be 'ready to do Justice to his Character if called on by the Admiralty'.[14] But in 1808, Mr William Dyker was employed as surgeon, a hard man by all accounts, Dr Magrath not being given the post until after Dyker's departure in September 1814. Instead, in October 1808, he was informed he had been appointed to Dartmoor occupying a lesser medical post. Later, he worked at Mill Prison in Plymouth, only making occasional visits to Dartmoor when extra help was needed.

The Napoleonic War created a demand for horses, and in April 1807 Messrs Isbell & Co were approached by a magistrate who wanted to know whether their horses employed in conveying materials to the prison site were liable to be impressed to convey regimental baggage and to perform statute labour on the roads. The Admiralty felt the horses should be exempt as the animals were already doing service for them.

A report on the progress of The Depot at Dartmoor in 1807 indicates that the Prisons were being slated, the Agent's and officers' houses were bare walls, the enclosed Barracks were still at foundation level, and the water courses had not been started. Mr Alexander's plan for thatched barns for housing peat was refused. Occupation by prisoners had been promised for Christmas 1807 but this was not to be. An estimated time of arrival was put back to summer 1808.

One reason for the delay was visitors. On 2 July 1807, the *Exeter Flying Post* reported that 'Whereas great hindrance and delay is experienced by the men employed on the works of the said prison, in consequence of visitors going through the same;- *It is ordered*, - That no persons be admitted but such as apply to the clerk of the works, who will give proper directions accordingly; and that none be admitted on Sundays'.

One of these visitors was artist Samuel Prout who made a series of sketches of the prison's progress in October 1806 and June 1807. Although seen as a hindrance by the workmen, he created an invaluable record of the building works.

It was in 1807 that Captain Isaac Cotgrave, a Royal Naval Officer, first appears on the scene. He was to be the first Prison Officer in Command, known as an Agent. On 21 September, while employed as Agent at Mill Prison in Plymouth, he wrote to the Admiralty asking if he could be considered for the position of Agent at Dartmoor when it opened. The Admiralty saw no reason to refuse this application and so he took up his new post within a few months. Although his employment at Mill Prison ended on 31 August 1808, his involvement with Dartmoor took effect months before.[15] Capt Cotgrave was considered a harsh man, if contemporary accounts from prisoners are to be believed.

From east to west, with Prison No.4 in the foreground. Part of an airing shed is on extreme left, and one of the polygonal stores is centre. Sketched by Samuel Prout on 3 June 1807.
Collection: Plymouth City Museum & Art Gallery.

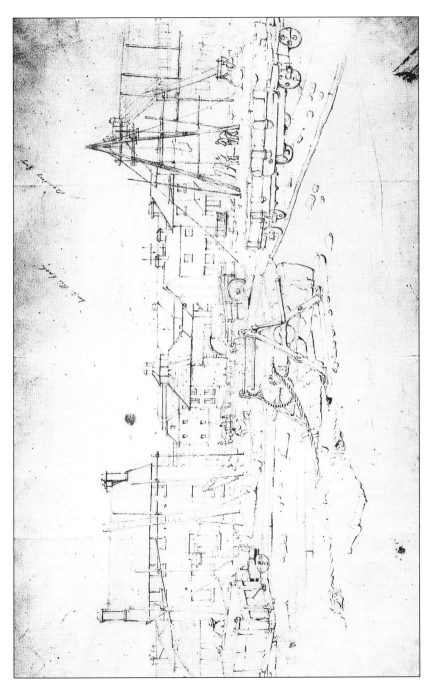

An unfinished sketch by Samuel Prout of Dartmoor Prison under construction. It is drawn from outside the complex looking past the surgeon's house towards one of the polygonal stores.
Collection: Plymouth City Museum & Art Gallery.

1808
The only items doing well were the fir trees

Building such a huge complex as the War Depot warranted a large workforce. However, the Board decided that no houses were to be built for the labourers and that they must find accommodation in the neighbourhood! This could not have been easy as Princetown was only just developing as a new settlement. A few cottages referred to as 'huts' in the records were already existing prior to the Depot. But Messrs Isbell & Co erected other 'huts' for their own workforce.[16]

Some Depot employees needed accommodation on the spot also, but their job did not justify their own house. For example, in September, the Board approved a wall to be put across the Hospital's C Ward for the seamstress' residence.

Obtaining quantities of fuel was of great importance and in June Capt Cotgrave was instructed by the Board to make enquiries concerning quantities and costs of turf. The costs turned out to be 7s 6d a journey (a 40 yard length of worked peat) if the peat was cut near the prison, and 10s if from further afield. Some of this peat may have come from Black Dunghill; a few of the remaining peat ties there measure 40 yards in length. Contemporary maps of the prison land show other peat areas within the prison boundary. The Board also needed to employ someone to take charge of the peat at the prison itself.

As well as peat, coal was used for fuel. On 20 September, Capt Cotgrave was told by the Board that the Depot was to procure both candles and coals, and that tenders should be invited. A few days later, they authorised the building of a coal house, shortly followed by an order of Sunderland coals from Tavistock - from Messrs Gill & Co. Some fuel also came from Plymouth. As an example of a personal coal allowance, the seamstress and the matron were permitted two bushels of coal a week each, together with 1lb of candles, between 1 October and 30 April, and one bushel of coal and ½ lb of candles between 1 May and 30 September.

Completing the buildings was not going too well. On 6 August, Mr Alexander sent the Board the 26th Report of Progress on the works at the Depot. Although most of the houses were finished, all the chimneys smoked, the concrete floors had blistered, the stone steps to the sentry boxes sited on peaked bastions of the inner granite boundary wall had partially collapsed due to careless workmanship, all the walls needed repointing, and the only items doing well were the fir trees (these later died)! So again occupation by prisoners was deferred, until 1809.

In the autumn, iron railings were erected from the Hospital to the Petty Officers' Prison. A turnkeys' lodge was to be built inside the Military Way (houses for them were also built outside the complex later on - these probably became Church Row). Capt Cotgrave was ordered to employ a plumber and glazier to reside at the Depot. This had not been done by late December, and the Board ordered Capt Cotgrave to put an advertisement in the Exeter and Plymouth papers. Eventually this post was filled in early 1809 by Mr Henry Rowe who was supplied with the implements he would need for his new job. He was also put in charge of the 'water courses' or leats.

As the autumn progressed, the records reflect a certain urgency on the part of the Board. Within the space of a few days, they had ordered padlocks for the Prison doors, all rubbish was to be removed, lamps were to be fixed 'immediately' and lit up with the soon to be provided lamp oil, alarm bells were to be fitted to the burying ground wall, Mr Pearse was to supply more candles, and Mr Billing the straw and birch brooms (both of Plymouth). Extra turf was to be provided by John Watts at 7s 6d per journey. This supply was to be used for airing the Prisons. This was lucky for John Watts as it would appear he had cut the peat 'in expectation of selling it to the Board'.[17] Shoes were ordered for the first consignment of prisoners, and 200 feather pillows were ordered for the Hospital.

In the meantime, Capt Cotgrave thought an engine house for the fire engine on order would be rather nice and told the Board as much. This did not go down too well and he was informed that Mr Alexander had made provision for the vehicle to stand in one corner of the covered arcade of the Hospital where it would be sheltered from the weather. Fire buckets were to be hung on nearby pegs.

Lamp glasses were ordered from Mr Huxham of Exeter. The cost of 13s each surprised the Board and they asked Mr Alexander what size they were and what kind of heads did they have to justify this price? His reply reveals that nothing much changes; the price included the packing cases and carriage.

Supplying bread for large numbers required appropriate facilities. At the end of November, Mr Alexander said the only ovens were in the houses of the Agent and the surgeon due to the price of fuel. He suggested 'a large Public Oven be set up which should be let for a competent rent'.[18] The Board approved this.

Bulk supplies were being ordered in preparation for the prisoners' arrival. On 14 October the Board ordered:

    5,000 hammocks
    5,000 palliasses
    5,000 bolsters
    5,000 blankets
    2,000 pairs of clews [the series of cords by which a hammock is suspended]

More and more Depot staff were being appointed. Mr John Arnold was to be a turnkey along with six others; Mr William Dovey, a dispenser (who later died and was replaced by Mr W.G. Winkworth); Mr John Buckingham, Capt Cotgrave's first clerk; Dr Magrath, part of the Hospital staff, and Mrs Mary Brooke, the seamstress who joined the Depot on 17 December.

The Barracks, still incomplete, initially did not have separate accommodation for the Barrack Master, Barrack Sergeant or Staff Sergeant. Mr Alexander seemed rather defensive about this when questioned, saying that the Dartmoor design was based on the plan for that at Haslar near Gosport in Hampshire. Furthermore, if the Barrack Board required additional accommodation, they should send in their own plans. He then suggested that one ward of the Depot's Hospital might be appropriated for the military, but in the meantime, the Barracks should be occupied by 250 or 300 men. Capt Cotgrave added to this by claiming that until the Barracks and the Prisons *were* occupied, they would always appear damp and unfinished.

At the end of December, the Board asked Mr Alexander when the Barracks *would* be finished. He told them the first week of January 1809, saying in the same letter that the grates were to come from Tavistock. The Barracks were situated to the south of the Depot, surrounded by an octagonal wall, the southern end having a rectangular extension. There were eleven main blocks plus a guard house, an octagonal wash house with four boilers and attached turf shed, privies and coal houses. A cook house, sleeping quarters, mess and stables, were also accommodated within the buildings.

Of the Prisons Nos 1 - 5, on 13 December Mr Alexander's agent, Mr Hemmingway, revealed that already the floors had become defective owing to the frequent fog. Should these floors give way when occupied, he commented, all the prisoners would have to be removed! Mr Alexander was sent to investigate. He reported that the floors of Prisons 1 and 5 'were but little defective and might be immediately occupied'.[19] The other bad floors, he felt, might be due to defective materials or bad workmanship and that he would investigate.

Investigation or not, the Board was anxious that the floor repairs were completed without delay, and Mr Hemmingway further pressed his view that the floors should be removed at once 'as neither the Plaister of Paris or Lime Ash will at all answer the intended purpose'.[20] However, Mr Alexander said no effectual measures could be taken to repair the defective plaster of the floors in winter.

In the meantime, Capt Cotgrave reported to the Board that some of the 'Huts' belonging to Messrs Isbell & Rowe 'be unfit for the residence of labourers or any Persons in the employ of the Department'. Their response is not recorded but it is likely to have been unsympathetic.[21]

The bad state of the roads was causing delays with the foot delivery of letters, and a lack of willing carriers. Indeed, 'the Woman who had hitherto conveyed the letters to & from Tavistock at 2d per letter would no longer continue this service without a stated salary'.[22] This salary was not forthcoming. Capt Cotgrave suggested that a horse could be kept at the Depot to go to and from Tavistock and Ashburton with letters, and that one of the labourers could be employed to do that. The Board agreed to this and authorised the purchase of a small horse and to hire a boy as messenger.

It is appropriate to mention here that the Plume of Feathers Inn had just been established. An insertion in the *Exeter Flying Post* on 15 September 1808 reads:

PRINCE'S PLUME INN, DARTMOOR

Robert Lane, having lately established the above inn, opposite the New Prison on the forest of Dartmoor, begs leave to assure his friends and the public that he will use his utmost endeavours to merit their countenance and support.

Although initially called the 'Prince's Plume Inn', it had become the Plume of Feathers Inn by 1809, with Richard Criper listed as the licensee.

And so 1808 ended with completion of the works nowhere in sight. It was towards the end of 1808 that the Board informed Capt Cotgrave that the name of the Depot was to change: 'The buildings under your Superintendance are to be called "Dartmoor Prison"'.[23] This was mostly adhered to in the written records with only the occasional reference to 'Depot' by a forgetful clerk. It would seem some headed paper retained 'Depot'; reprinting would have been an additional cost to bear.

The Plume of Feathers, opened as an inn by Robert Lane in 1808. *Kingway.*

1809
Arrival of the French Prisoners of War - 'This melancholy sight strikes the view and conveys to the soul a kind of bitterness'

It is often claimed that the building of the prison complex was virtually finished in 1809. But this is a far cry from reality. Suppliers also had to be found for the time when the Barracks were fully staffed and the prison fully occupied by prisoners. Contractors were needed for food provisions and came from a large catchment area; they had to pay a bond of £3,000. The expense of victualling each man depended on different contracts; 'we have had it as low as sixpence, and as high as eight-pence'.[24] The Board decided the best way to get both goods and prisoners to the prison was via Lopwell Quay. However, Capt Cotgrave had great misgivings about this and, in January, said that the Quay was inconvenient for the landing of prisoners and stores due to the intricacy of navigation and the want of carriages. But the Board would not give way and instructed Capt Cotgrave to advertise in local papers for tenders to convey stores from Lopwell Quay to Dartmoor Prison. They further asked him to find out the charge per lighterage from Plymouth to the Quay, how much quicker it would be via Lopwell Quay rather than overland from Plymouth, and the costs per ton from Plymouth to the prison.

Capt Cotgrave replied that although five or six miles of land travel would be saved, navigation to Lopwell Quay was very difficult, there was no storehouse there, no one to look after the stores, and bad roads to the prison.

In the meantime, the Barracks and the Prison floors *still* needed to be sorted out. Mr Alexander was ordered to take immediate measures for putting this in hand. But the weather intervened. On 17 January Capt Cotgrave informed the Board that the whole area was covered in snow and that frost had stopped the entire supply of water with the exception of a spring supplying his house by the means of a small pipe, and a similar spring and pipe in the Barrack yard.

The situation must have eased within a few days as Mr Alexander was able to inform the Board that a Mr Banks of Nottingham was to visit Dartmoor Prison on 20 January to examine the Prison floors and that he was an expert in the laying of ones made from cement. The advice Mr Banks gave confirmed that the cause of disrepair was the weather and 'fogs'. He suggested another type of floor which, Mr Alexander assured the Board, would succeed.

In addition to this, a report of late January revealed that 'drains and gutters are incomplete, and a great Quantity of Rubbish and large Stones remain to be removed from the Prison Yard & Military Way, that a Gate is wanting to the Burial Ground and the reservoir and Ponds require to be cleaned out'.[25] Mr Alexander was ordered to see to these works as soon as possible. He also sent the Board a plan for the Officers' accommodation (he must have felt compelled to listen to the Barrack Board's complaint!) which is likely to have been the Duchy Hotel, built for such a function. William Stocker appears in records as the first landlord in 1810. Another oven for the baking of bread for the workmen was approved by the Board in April.

Some of Messrs Isbell & Co's 'huts' for the workforce were habitable and men were permitted to continue living in them for a while, including Anthony Cooper who wrote specifically to the Board to allow him to remain. He was told he could stay until May when a Board member would visit the prison. Other huts were being built, including one for Mr Bennett who was told 'to take care that it be a proper distance from the Walls'.[26]

The Duchy Hotel, built for Officers of the militia.

The ground around Dartmoor Prison was rather barren, and seeds to plant in the vicinity were supplied by John Veitch at a cost of £102 3s. Mr Veitch had established a well respected nursery at Budlake near Killerton, Exeter. Also, kitchen garden plots were, in February, chosen by Capt Cotgrave for the use of Officers employed at the prison. Labourers and turnkeys were prepared to do occasional gardening work until the prisoners arrived.

On 18 April, Capt Cotgrave was told that 2,500 prisoners would be arriving at Dartmoor Prison on 1 May, each bringing with them a new hammock and clews. However, their arrival was suspended because, although the first Barrack Master had been appointed by 6 March, the Barracks themselves were in no fit state. Also, part of a wall had sunk (into a boggy spot probably!) and was having to be rebuilt.

Items were continuing to be ordered including lamp oil from London, bedding, tables and forms (benches) for the Hospital's open-plan wards. The non-arrival of the fire engine was of some concern and, in response to enquiries, the manufacturers Messrs Hadley & Simpson assured the Board it was nearly ready and would be sent within a few days. It was dispatched on 20 May 'by waggon from the Saracen's Head Inn, Friday Street, Cheapside & should arrive at Tavistock in 8 days from that time'.[27] Better late than never!

The matron was allowed a 'cradle', hospital bedding, shirts, blankets and a rug, as were sick prisoners. In addition, she was given two deal tables, two ruck bottom chairs, a fender, a set of fire irons, a candlestick, a hearthbrush and a pair of snuffers.

Arrival of the French

On 17 May Capt Cotgrave learnt that the Plymouth Agent, Capt Rogers, was to send 2,500 French prisoners to Dartmoor Prison immediately. They were to march overland and not via Lopwell Quay (it seems Capt Cotgrave had won this battle) and they arrived on 24 May. Nearing Princetown, they followed the track which was to become known as Frenchmen's Road, which went towards North Hessary Tor before descending to the prison. Their march to Dartmoor must

'Parcere Subjectis' inscribed on the outer entrance gate. *Valentine.*

have been an amazing sight; not only were there men on foot, but cart loads of baggage. 'The baggage of the crew of the Beinfasant [sic] alone occupied 35 carts'.[28]

By mid-September, the numbers of prisoners had risen to 5,100, the others arriving in the preceding months. Hemery[29] claims that prisoners had an overnight stop at Durance Farm near Meavy, but there is no evidence of this in the records, and prisoners Charles Andrews and Joseph Velpey report their marches as having been accomplished in one day.

On their arrival the prisoners were greeted with the words PARCERE SUBJECTIS on the gateway - 'Spare the Vanquished' - taken from Virgil's 'Hae tibi erunt artes: pacisque imponere morem, Parcere subjectis et debellare superbos'. Translated, this means 'Let those be your arts: to impose peace, to spare the vanquished and abase the proud'. This inscription was, according to Thomson, repaired by the French in 1812. As seen, Catel's first impression of the prison was not favourable: 'This melancholy sight strikes the view and conveys to the soul a kind of bitterness'.[30]

Some prisoners were of nationalities other than French. The Dutch ships seized by the British (Holland was in league with Napoleon) housed Eurasians, Malays, and Chinese, all in the service of the Dutch East India Company. In Catel's account of his experiences in Dartmoor Prison, he claimed that the French were a minority amongst the prisoners; he lists Spaniards, Portuguese,

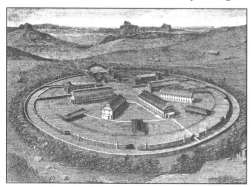

'Perspective View of the War Prison near Tor Royal' c.1809 by Samuel Prout. *Courtesy Ron Joy.*

Italians, Swiss, Germans, Prussians, Poles, Russians, Austrians, 'Piemontais', Saxons, Belgians, 'Flamards', Dutch, Danish, Swedes, Asiatics, Americans and Africans.

Women and children also were found among the prisoners arriving in 1809. They were put on a cart, the women given 1 guinea, and taken back to Plymouth for repatriation to France.

The Prisons themselves in which the French men were to be confined, although new, were far from comfortable.

Doors at each end of Prisons 1-5 gave access to these two storey affairs, with attics and clerestories intended for use as promenades in wet weather. Each floor was one large room with concrete/plaster floors and, according to Mr Alexander, 'about 170 or 180 feet long, by 33 or 34 broad'.[31] Prison No.1 was supposedly 16 bays long and Nos 2-5 were 12 bays.[32] They had internal broad granite steps at each end to the upper floors. The windows were two feet wide, unglazed and heavily barred. About 500 prisoners were reputedly confined on each floor which had two alleyways from end to end dividing their hammocks. These were hung from sturdy timbers or metal columns in tiers, the numbers of which vary from three to eight, according to the views of different authors. However, the contemporary accounts of Commissioner Capt James Bowen and Dr Baird maintain that the hammocks were hung in two tiers.[33] They were two or three feet apart. Conditions must have been far from comfortable, due largely to overcrowding and everything that brings with it. Tallow candles and oil lamps were the only light source after dark, and in the surviving Prison No.4 (originally No.3 until two other Prisons were built in 1812), scorch marks together with hammock ringbolt marks, are still visible on the roof timbers. The stoves on which food items could be cooked had flues running to the nearest windows.

Thriving in this fug of steam and human warmth were lice and bedbugs for extra company. The prisoners were also presented with a set of about 18 regulations which included the requirement that Prisons 'shall be swept, scraped and washed by the Prisoners in rotation as often and in such manner as the Agent shall order';[34] even if adhered to, the vermin situation retained its status quo! Stone scuppers can be seen on the external walls of Prison No.4 where water from washing down the floors could escape. The initial influx of prisoners were put in Prisons No.1 and 2, but those in the latter were soon moved to No.5.

Prisoners were also provided with 'common soldiers bedding': one hammock, one blanket, 1 horse-rug, and a bed containing four pounds of flock. Every 18 months prisoners also received one yellow 'round-about' jacket (with the letters TO TO - propably for Transport Office - printed on them), one pair of pantaloons, a waistcoat of the same materials and a woollen cap. Every 9 months, they were given a pair of shoes and a shirt. Surprisingly, they were allowed to keep their foils (swords) at first.

At this point, it might be appropriate to explain how the French prisoners divided themselves into various social strata. Thomson gives a good concise description which one can do no better than quote:

"'Les Lords' consisted of men of good family who were drawing on their bankers or receiving regular remittances from home; 'Les Labourers' were those who added to their rations by the manufacture of articles for sale in the market. 'Les Indifferents' did nothing but lounge about the yards, and had to content themselves with the Government rations. 'Les Minables' were the gamblers and hatchers of mischief'.[35]

Here were also 'Les Kaiserlics' who were considered nearly the lowest of the low - but not quite. Each group elected a leader known as a 'Commissaire'.

And then there were 'Les Romains'. Authors often claim these numbered between 250 and 500 but records indicate that at one time, in 1813, they numbered 1,400. These men were a breed apart! They were hardened gamblers whose lifestyle became so base that they were banished to

Prison No.4; the privy block would have been on the end wall under which the foul leat would have passed.
Elisabeth Stanbrook.

the roof space or 'cockloft', originally intended as a promenade area for times of wet weather. Les Romains, or 'Romans', evolved because, as gambling swept the prison, this group of men did not stop when funds ran out, but continued to gamble their bedding and clothing, and exchanged food for tobacco. Hence they lived and slept in a naked state and could be found during daytime hours scavenging for food in the rubbish heaps. Surgeon William Dyker remembered '...there was a merchant about the prison who sold potatoes by the halfpennyworths and pennyworths at a time, and they would frequently beg halfpence and pence from the country people who came to market, and with the fruits of their begging they would buy these potatoes of the merchant, and this person sold them in a raw state'.[36] They were pariahs of the whole prisoner community and consequently shunned.

Thus a camaraderie grew up amongst the 'Romans' who, out of their state of filthy chaos, managed to find some sort of order. Like the other groups, they elected a 'General' to take charge, and each of their cocklofts became known as 'Le Capitole'. They annoyed other prisoners so much that, in 1812, they were all confined to Prison No.4 (formerly No.3) which had walls built to separate it and the adjoining yards from the other prisoners.

Between 1809 and 1814 there was also a Freemasons Lodge called 'De la Réunion'.

It is the American prisoner Charles Andrews' account of prison life that gives details of required prisoner of war rations, although they vary slightly from those given by Thomson. Contractors for victualling the prisoners had to provide:

For 5 days: 1½ lbs coarse brown bread
    ½ lb beef
    ⅓ oz barley
    ⅓ oz salt
    ⅓ oz onions
    1lb turnips

For 2 days: 1½ lbs coarse bread
    1lb pickled fish
    sufficient quantities of coal to cook it.

The allowance for prisoners confined in the Hospital was more generous, apparently.

The cooking of the food in large copper boilers, some with a capacity of 300 gallons, was as follows: 'On beef days, the whole is thrown into a large copper, when it is sufficiently boiled, the bone is taken out, and each mess [group of men eating together], consisting of six, receives twenty-seven ounces of beef, and one gallon and one pint of soup.

'On the fish days, every mess boiled their potatoes and fish in a net made of rope-yarn, that they might have it separately to themselves; after it was boiled, it was taken up in wooden buckets, with which each mess were provided; and each prisoner, being also furnished with a wooden spoon, sets round the bucket, on the wet floor, and makes a fierce attack'.[37] According to Catel, this food distribution was announced by the blowing of a cow's horn.[38]

The food was not always of the quality required. Later, in December, Capt Cotgrave suspected 'bull beef' instead of beef had been provided. The Board ordered him to send a 'proper Person' to attend at the slaughtering of cattle by the contractors Agent 'whom you will call upon to state to you how long, previous to the killing of the Cattle, he considers it necessary for them to be castrated in order to entitle the Beef to be what Butchers in general admit as, according to the Terms of the Contract, "not Bull Beef"'.[39]

By September, more than three years since the laying of the foundation stone, and with so many prisoners having been received, one might think that the end of the building work was in sight. But no! Consequently Messrs Joliffe & Banks were given permission to employ prisoners on construction work inside. It was not until mid-September that the floors in the Prison blocks were finally finished.

The erection of a partition was found be to necessary in the dispenser's store to separate clean and dirty linen; a 'dead house' (ie mortuary) was found to be badly sited and had to be demolished and rebuilt outside the north prison walls at a cost of £35; more sentry boxes were to be erected; the attics in the Prisons, which were being used as stores (instead of the intended 'promenades'), were now to be hung with hammocks from stanchions and specially bought

Detail of one of the upright timbers in the roof of Prison No.4; note the hammock ringbolt and scorch marks.
© *Crown copyright NMR.*

The attic or 'cockloft' which survives in Prison No.4. The original uprights are now flanked with modern wooden supports but the scorch marks and hammock ringbolt marks can still be seen.
© *Crown copyright NMR.*

timbers which had to be installed - by the prisoners who were employed as carpenters and paid 6d a day. The surviving Prison No.4 attic provides a good example of their work; it

'has queenposts with expanded heads which support a collar on which there is a short kingpost. Above the lower collar there is another collar which is constructed of two pieces on either side of the kingpost. The rafters for the upper part of the roof spring from the top of this upper collar allowing a short clerestory to be created between the two collars. This clerestory was presumably barred but unglazed... There are small princess posts on the outside of the queenposts. The major joints of the roof have straps.'[40]

The Barracks needed additional work, and the walkways under the Hospital were to be gravelled at an estimated cost of £20. The prisoners themselves were also permitted to erect some fireplaces in an open yard, and the Petty Officer prisoners were allowed to buy turf.

An entry in the records for 19 September further shows that:

flooring of the turnkey's lodge was to be planked; the general cook room was to be laid with broad stone and its door to be made within the prison railings, in order to keep the prisoners within the prison, but the door of it to be kept locked except when the cooks were using it; a doorway was to be made through the cross walls for the convenience of the guard passing round the prison within the inner wall, forming the Military Way, and the key was to be kept by an Officer of the guard; sentry boxes were to be placed opposite the cross walls on the platform.

43 lamps were to be installed; shutes were to carry off water from the cook house, and a hole or holes were to be made to enable two or more cooks to serve at the same time; the lubber boards were to be made broader so that one would cover another and be made more moveable; holes were to be made so that the Petty Officers could purchase articles in the common market place - but they were to be shut securely at other times; iron grates were to be fixed in Prison privies; an additional chimney and fireplace was to be built in the mens' guard room; floors and close shutters were needed for the straw house to the north of the reservoir, tables and boiler covers were to be ordered for the cook room; a stove was to be installed in the seamstress's bedroom and a place for coals, and shelves were to be made; turf sheds for two clerks were to be erected; an awning or shed was to be put up for prisoners when receiving their provisions; a Hospital store room was to be built under the south east end of the Hospital arcade and the fire engine removed to a small enclosure near the inner entrance gate; an apartment for bedding and clothing of the sick prisoners was to be made; an operation room (about 12 feet square) was to be built; a small bulkhead was needed for the Hospital turnkey's room as it was exposed to wind and weather; a thatched cart lodge was to be erected outside the entrance to the prison for the market people to leave their carts under during market hours; drying sheds for the Hospital were to be built and its wash house was to be enlarged.

To oversee these extensive alterations and building requirements, Mr John Walters from Ilfracombe was employed as Foreman of the Works. He was paid 2 guineas a week and given 10s 6d lodging money until an apartment could be provided for him. He was also allowed 6d per mile travelling expenses from Ilfracombe to Dartmoor Prison, which came to £1 9s (58 miles). To assist him in his work, he was allowed to employ French prisoners.

A much needed carpenter's and joiner's shop had to be built to cope with these works and the need for two new cook rooms was also suggested, with the present one being turned into a guard room. With the Barracks still unfinished, the Petty Officers' Prison was to be prepared for the reception of troops. Airing sheds were also requested (the first ones had been pulled down!) and a division was to be built across the prison yard. In November, a slaughterhouse was ordered as were houses for drying linen in December.[41]

The slaughterhouse had been requested by General England who told the Board that it was very inconvenient having no such facility at the Depot for use of the military. Consequently, Capt Cotgrave was told to look into the feasibility of providing one for them. The plan and estimate provided by Mr Walters was approved and he was ordered to have one built at a cost of £370. The site of the slaughterhouse is where the present school now stands; a stream, to become known as the 'Butchery Stream', which rose not far from Meavy Head, flowed past the building carrying the effluent via a small pool into the foul leat (see Appendix I).

The need for stone was never ending and Messrs Isbell & Co found themselves being issued with a writ by Sir Massey Lopes for extracting granite from Walkhampton Common without his permission; he was awarded £500 damages.

Despite all these additions and alterations, it would seem that the first phase of the prison, as designed by Mr Alexander, was completed by 15 December as he wrote to the Board saying that he would no longer require the services of his agent, Mr Hemmingway.

In the meantime, staff were continuing to be appointed. These included Mr Edmund Pearse (senior hospital mate and a French interpreter), Mr William Gray (acting surgeon at the Hospital until Mr Dyker, on board a ship in the Ganges, could get back to the prison), Mr Nathan G. Poulden (who quickly replaced Mr Gray), and various turnkeys, stewards and clerks to be paid 1s 3d a day: Messrs Frederick Gottlieb, Richard Hamden, Thomas Dyer, John Newcombe, Samuel Barrett, Martin Maynard, John Morgan, James Cleave Madge, John Crispin, James Carley and John Duncan.

Also employed, as already mentioned, were the prisoners themselves. In June, a French surgeon was taken on as assistant to Mr Dovey and later, Mr Winkworth, at 1s a day; in July, many prisoners were employed to pick hair (for bedding stuffing) at 3d a day; August saw prisoners being paid 9d a day for attending to the lamps; carpenters for building work were paid 6d a day.

Orders for supplies continued prolifically. Dr Magrath's order alone in early June contained numerous items including:

Bolus[?] Paper - 2 Reams	Gallipots - 2 [?]	Glass Funnels - 2
Brown Paper - 2 Reams	Graduated Measures - 2 [?]	Tin Funnels - 6
Bladders - 1 dozen	Taper - 2 Pieces	Hammer - 1
White leather - 4 skins	Pins - 2 lbs	Mistal[?] Ladle - 1
Twine - 6 Balls	Issue Pens - 300 [?]	Thermometer - 1
Large Corks - 2 [?]	Cork Screws - 2	Oil Cloths for saving the Beds
Pill Boxes Sorted - 6 Papers	Large Scales & Weights - 1 set	- 6
Leeches - 1 dozen	Small Scales & Weights - ditto	Crutches - 12 pairs
Large Pewter Syringes - 2 [?]	Edinburgh Dispenscitory[?] - 1	Phial Corks - 6 [?]

Messrs Gill & Co of Tavistock were to supply coals at 34s 6d a quarter. More coals and candles were needed for the Hospital department, as were several items of furniture such as chairs for prison staff and for the Barracks department. Turnkeys were allowed 2¹/₂ bushels of coal per week in winter. Coffins were also ordered. In June, Dr Magrath was given permission to order two dozen from a Mr Luckraft. In July, Mr John Martin of Tavistock, eager it would seem to make a profit on his own coffin-making business, offered to supply the prison with them at 18s each. This was rejected outright by the Board as their current supplier was charging them only 7s 9¹/₂d each.

5,100 prisoners required huge supplies of clothing and bedding. The summer, autumn and winter of 1809 saw large orders being placed for such items:

19 June	- 3,000 suits of clothing
1 July	- 1,000 hats
15 August	- 500 hammocks (at 6s 3d each)
29 August	- 3,000 hammocks
	2,000 palliasses (at 3s 10d each)
	3,000 washed blankets
26 September	- 4,000 blankets (at 4s 10d each)
8 December	- 6,000 coverlets

plus numerous bolster cases at 11¹/₂d each.

Ordered for the prisoners in the Hospital were: bed cases (mattress covers?) at 9s 2d each, bolster cases at 2s 1d each, pillow cases at 1s ¹/₂d each and numerous blankets at 6s each.

Junk (old rope) from Portsmouth Dockyard was ordered from which some of the hammock clews were to be made.

Only two months after their arrival, some of the French prisoners had already sold or destroyed their bedding - the 'Romans' no doubt. They were put on short allowance and not given replacements until their health required it!

The prison was, of course, now patrolled by troops. What was expected of them? Colonel Wood of the East Middlesex Regiment explained:

'The duty consists in mounting a large guard, consisting of 120 privates, and which furnished 40 sentries. The frequent recurrence of the duty will of course depend upon the strength of the garrison. But at Dartmoor that number can never be increased above a certain amount, because there are only accommodations for a certain number of troops, and the number of sentries can never be diminished, because it is necessary to surround one of the walls entirely with sentries. This observation applies merely to the number of sentries necessary to keep a look out; the strength of the force to be kept at such a station must depend upon the persons whose duty it is to restrain'.[42]

He went on to add;

'the duty of Dartmoor has always been done by a detachment of infantry sent from the garrison of Plymouth, amounting to between 550 and 600 men; and it has been the practice to relieve these detachments once in three months. It is certainly desirable that the soldiers should not be called upon to mount guard more frequently than every third night; because this is a duty in which extreme vigilance is necessary, and it is hardly possible to expect that degree of vigilance which would prevent the escape of any person detained in the prison, if the soldiers rest is broken more frequently than every third night'.[43]

Architect Daniel Alexander provides some additional information about the two granite perimeter walls and the iron palisade; the palisade

The outer boundary wall from inside the prison. *Elisabeth Stanbrook.*

'was eight feet high, and very difficult to scale... The external boundary wall was ten feet, [raised to 12 feet in 1812] and the internal fourteen... The walls were constructed with points resembling bastions, so as that the centinels [sic] could flank themselves every way, and guard the prison in proportion with a fewer number of men; the space between the inner boundary wall and the palisade, was termed No-man's-land: it was dug up, and planted with potatoes, and it was a fine of imprisonment for any prisoner to be found between the palisade and this inner boundary wall, except those who were at work'.[44]

It would seem that root crops did well at the prison as they were also grown with great success in the Agent's garden.

Escapes were to be a frequent occurrence at the prison. One tragic incident was recorded on 26 October in the *Exeter Flying Post*: 'Several French prisoners at Dartmoor lately got beyond the boundary of the prison walls, into the military pass, an alarm was immediately given, when an officer's servant of the Royal Lancashire Militia unfortunately came without his usual accoutrements, and being mistaken for one of the Frenchmen, was stabbed by his comrade in so desperate a manner, that he expired two days after'.

Shortly after this, a Mr Roberts fixed alarm bells on the prison walls at a cost of £37 19s 9d. Of this, Catel says that an iron wire, suspended by springs about 15 or 20 centimetres from the top supported small bells at intervals and any escape attempt caused them to ring, thus alerting the sentries. He also says that the cast iron railings were surmounted every 5 metres by reflecting mirrors which were cleaned every day. Every now and then, around the whole of each building, other mirrors were similarly placed and were very precisely lit every evening.

The market, within the confines of a special square in the prison, was of benefit to both local traders and prisoners. The former sold various permitted items at a fixed rate (to ensure fair trading) including fruit, vegetables, fish, tobacco, tea, coffee etc. The latter sold goods of their own manufacture. Some of these items survive today and bear testimony to the skilled craftsmanship of many French prisoners. Intricate models of ships and a guillotine etc made from beef bones and hair, carved wooden models and plaited hair decorations were all offered for sale. Items made from straw, such as ladies hats, were initially sold, but this was soon prohibited 'on account of their plaiting the straw, which was an injury to the manufacturers; the people of Bristol memorialised against it'.[45]

Wooden model of a French trial scene, made by a French
prisoner of war.
Oxford University Press.

Bone model of a guillotine, made by French prisoners
of war.
Oxford University Press.

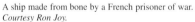

A ship made from bone by a French prisoner of war.
Courtesy Ron Joy.

A small intricately-made dominoes set, made from bone
by a French prisoner of war.
Courtesy P. Hamilton-Leggett.

At first, in accordance with the regulations, the markets were held from 9am to noon everyday except Sunday, but in later years, the hours appear to have been extended to most of the day. Occasionally markets were cancelled due to misdemeanours, for example, upon the discovery of homemade daggers in August.

With so many people confined in the Prisons, it is not surprising to find that disease was fairly commonplace, spreading rapidly among the under-nourished prisoners. In November, there was a measles epidemic which lasted until April 1810, discussed in the next chapter. It was thought to have been introduced by invalid prisoners from the West Indies.

Ordered for Mr Winkworth's dispensary in November were:

1 large kettle or boiler	1 candlestick
1 gallon saucepan	1 hair sieve
1 long-handled scrubbing brush	2 keys cuchs(?)
1 fender	1 large knife
1 sifter	1 mop
1 door mat	

Some accounts recorded for 1809 were:

William Huxham	£12	14s	2d
Mount Foundry & Co	£297	17s	11d
Mount Foundry & Co	£52	3s	9d
William Wells	£136	12s	4d
John Billing	£39	10s	

And so 1809 ends with the first influx of prisoners of war having been incarcerated inside an incomplete, cold and damp complex, soon to be rife with disease, and which they themselves were expected to help finish.

1810
Disease, deterioration, disposal of 'filth' and demolition of labourers huts

The measles epidemic had taken a firm grip on the prisoners. It was found too difficult to isolate them from the healthy ones in Prisons 1 & 5 and, despite French prisoners being considered as sentries to keep both parties apart, the sick were eventually installed in Prison No.2. By 2 February, their numbers had reached 800 and Dr Baird, the Inspector of H.M. Hospitals and Prison Hospitals, said they could accept no more sick prisoners from Plymouth. He was permitted to order 2 ozs soap per sick prisoner per week, and medicines were ordered from the Royal Hospital in Plymouth.

Such were the numbers that General England ordered that the Petty Officers' Prison should be given over to the Hospital department so that it could be used as a hospital to contain the fever; the Petty Officers did not occupy it until December. Two additional assistant surgeons were to be employed. The dying could expect little comfort from their doctor, if a contemporary account is to be believed. It would appear that Mr Dyker would order a coffin to be placed within sight of a dying man so that he could observe its effect on the unfortunate invalid. Death registers reveal there were about 500 deaths from this epidemic.

The local Coroner was kept so busy that he complained that the jurors pay should be increased from 8d to 1s as many had to travel long distances and were farmers and 'artificers'.[46]

All contagious material had to be destroyed and so many items of hospital laundry needed drying that they had to be sent to Plymouth for that purpose. Sending them to Tavistock, which was nearer, was deemed impracticable because 'Tavistock is a place not at all exempted from rain'.[47] Speaking later, Dr Baird complained that 'there was not a bed, or particle of bedding, that was not in an impure state, I could not get any thing purified and dried at the moor, so that I was obliged to send all the hospital things, so rendered impure, to Plymouth Hospital, to be washed and cleaned.'[48]

These difficulties made the medical staff review their facilities, and Mr Dyker said that the drying house, still

The former Petty Officers' Prison, sometimes used to house the militia and even sick prisoners. © *Crown copyright NMR.*

not built, was needed, a request readily agreed to by the Board. They also cited the need for a larger wash house and a store room for the foul clothing.

The airing sheds were to be rebuilt to a design by Mr Adams the surveyor, adjoining the prison. Dr Baird said: 'the then superintendent of the prison thought those sheds unnecessary; and they were taken down; the consequence was, that the prisoners hammocks hung in the prison constantly day and night... the filth and confined air had a considerable share in producing the sickness'.[49] Having to keep their hammocks inside, the prisoners 'nailed them up in the shape of a coffin and there they remained night and day'.[50] Initially the new airing shed was to be 100 feet in length, but this was changed to two of 50 feet in length. From the plan of 1810, it appears that four airing sheds were finally agreed upon.

On 24 February Capt Cotgrave sent the Board Mr Billing's estimate of £250 for the drying house or, if double the size, £450, to which the Board agreed. This drying house was nearly not to be. On 28 February, Mr Walters was informed that the difficulties in obtaining local workmen and materials meant that the drying house was not feasible. However, by May, the Board had changed their minds and authorised the building. But they presented further difficulties when Mr Walters needed a bricklayer to erect the flues. They wanted the mason currently employed by them to do this work but, as Capt Cotgrave had to explain to them, although the mason was good at his work, not only was he fully employed building a slaughterhouse, but the flues needed someone who was acquainted with building a drying house. Reluctantly the Board had to give way.

Fumigation and whitewashing the prison buildings with lime after the sick prisoners had been removed was ordered. Ninety of them were discharged to Plymouth in March. In the meantime, the healthy prisoners tried their luck at requesting a billiards table - which the Board refused!

Under John Walters the building work continued, although Mr Hemmingway was rather surprised to have his employment terminated, not having been informed of this by Mr Alexander.

As with several buildings already constructed, the cook house was considered to have been wrongly sited as it was too far from the prison. In February it was decided that each Prison should have its own cook house as well, rather than the two new ones suggested in 1809, and an estimate for these was sent by Mr Walters to the Board. It was not until May that the go-ahead for these kitchens was given, and Capt Cotgrave was able to order blocks and rope for scaffolding. Horses and carts were also ordered as needed. John Wethams' plan of 1812 show the kitchens on the inner ends of each of the Prisons (see p.49).

The idea for additional Barracks for 500 men was mooted in February by the Board. Capt Cotgrave suggested the most suitable place was the burying ground and that the dead could be buried elsewhere! Although the Board agreed to this, it would seem that this did not happen.

Flag pavements were to be placed at doors to the Prisons, and a hearth stone was required for the temporary hospital in the Petty Officers' Prison. The privy floors were found to be defective and the Board gave instructions for them to be paved with moor stone by the prisoners. The mason expressed some doubt as to the ease with which the prisoners could work this stone, but the Board rather unsympathetically said that if he had difficulty in instructing them to do this, another mason must be found. The water courses were also in a state of disrepair and the seamstress needed a window and a chimney in her apartment because she complained that it was too dark and smoky from the stove.

The slaughterhouse was still under construction during May, the large stones from the moor supplied by Mr Richard Hall. The mason was so busy trying to get it finished that he refused to help with the building of the drying houses. The slaughterhouse was not finished until 18 September, ten months after General England had first requested it. It was offered for letting, and Mr Hutton, who had the contract for the prison Hospital(!), offered £30 per annum, which was accepted.

Mr John Kroger of Plymouth was supplying the prison with bread and biscuits and showed great interest in building more bakeries on Dartmoor. But in January, the public oven on the Tavistock Road had been leased to Messrs Hagerman, Drake and Twynham and rented out to Mr Thorne, a miller from Tavistock for £30 p.a.; he was recommended for this by Major Corbutt. Mr Hagerman (who supplied flour from Plymouth) had apparently offered to rent the bakehouse in Two Bridges Road but by May it had been leased to Mr James Cooper for £1,700.[51]

Works already carried out were deteriorating. By April, Capt Cotgrave had to report that much of the pointing had been destroyed by frost, and that cement, supposedly sent to the prison for repairs, was nowhere to be found. In addition to this, the rotten mortar was causing problems with the 'Black Hole' or Cachot. This was a very small structure close to the Military Way in which prisoners whose misdemeanour was of a serious nature were incarcerated. Regulation 6 stipulated that 'Any Prisoner who shall be taken attempting to escape, shall be put in the Black Hole for ten Days, and shall lose his turn of Exchange'.[52] To be put on 2/3 rations as well was not unusual.

In late March, Capt Cotgrave had expressed concerns that prisoners in the Black Hole were 'constantly committing Depredations'[53] and that three had broken out through the wall and had mixed with other prisoners. By August, the number of escapes had increased, and escapees were having to be held in a guard house.

Capt Cotgrave told the Board that a stronger Cachot with larger stones must be built and, on 16 August, Mr Walters submitted a plan and estimate for £210. On 29 September, they approved this, ordering that it should be built as near to the guard house as possible, and *not* in the middle of the Prison yard; airholes were to be close to the roof.

The building of the Cachot was not started immediately. It was not until December that horses were hired for the conveyance of stone to be used. Some of this stone weighed a ton a piece and 'were carted to the spot to form the floor; the walls and the vaulted roof were made of dressed granite. When finished it measured 20 feet square inside. The only windows were two openings under the eaves 6 inches by 4. The door was iron plated on both sides with a wicket 8 inches square through which the rations could be passed. It had no function of any kind, not even straw to lie upon'.[54] This description is similar to Catel's and the measurements may have been copied by Thomson. In fact, the Cachot was an oblong building and measured approximately 20 feet by 33 feet internally. Catel's description may have been of the first Cachot; he was probably among some of the first prisoners and would have remembered it.

In mid-June Mr Walters informed the Board that the number of buildings required were too many to be completed that year and asked which ones were the most important. The answer came back as the cook house (which they decided to keep) and drying house, but that it was preferable that all buildings were completed even if it meant employing more English masons and

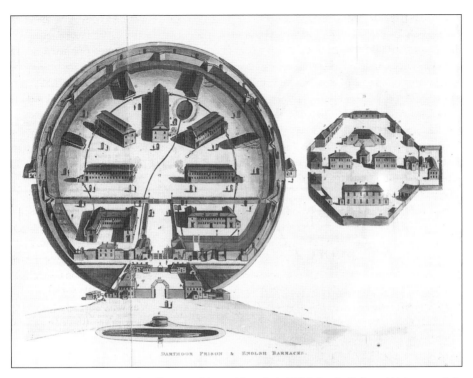

Plan of Dartmoor Prison and Barracks in 1810, before the Cachot and kitchens were built.
Westcountry Studies Library, Devon Library and Information Services.

bricklayers. Within a few days, William May had been employed as a slater at £1 11s 6d per week. Three boys were also taken on at 6d a day to convey tools to and from the smith for the French prisoners.

Prisoners employed in manual labour were being supplied with beer and Mr Walters asked if the French prisoners employed as carpenters could have a small amount as well as the masons. Initially the Board agreed to this but, when Mr Walters asked if the prisoners digging stone for buildings could have beer as their need was even greater than the carpenters, they said all masons and stone diggers could have beer, but *not* carpenters!

Now that the buildings designed by Mr Alexander had been erected, the iron railway constructed to transport material around the site was no longer in use. Mr Bough wrote to Capt Cotgrave offering to buy the rails at £6 per ton, but this was refused as the building work was continuing and it was possible the railway might still be needed.

By October the Prisons were full and the Board was wondering how many more prisoners could be accommodated without having to put them in the attics. The buildings had been too crowded last winter and they felt it must not happen again.

A natural outcome of so many people was what was often referred to as 'filth'. Word got round neighbouring farms that quantities were rather large (too large for the foul leat which carried away waste from the Prisons), and in May, Mr Hullett applied to the prison to buy the manure at a rate of 9d per load. The Board accepted this at first but, realising other interested parties might be prepared to pay more, invited tenders for it to include ashes and soil. Tenders were to be for a certain rate per cart or wagon load and for a period of 12 months. Early July saw Revd James Holman Mason successfully tender for the manure at 10^1/$_4$d a cartload, the cart to be drawn by two horses. Catel recalls a man with a two-horse cart coming daily to the prison to collect the filth ('ordure') from the courtyard. Revd Mason had taken a lease on Crockern Cottage in 1808 and held several hundred acres of land from the Duchy of Cornwall in the area north of Two Bridges; another individual intent on taming Dartmoor into productive farmland. He was vicar of Treneglos and Warbstow in Cornwall from 1804 to 1848 and also of Widecombe-in-the-Moor from 1815 to 1860.

Escaping prisoners were an occupational hazard and Capt Cotgrave was permitted to buy a horse especially for the pursuit of escapees. He also wanted two or three braces of common pistols, costing between £4 4s and £4 14s 6d, but eventually opted for one pair plus a holster.

Staff and workmen employed at the prison were not above accepting bribes from prisoners or from selling them illicit goods. In April, Mr Newcombe, a turnkey, was accused by medical staff Dyker and Dickson of 'Traffic in Wine & Beer'.[55] It would appear that Newcombe was suspended from duty because the Board wrote to him at a London address ordering his return to duty at Dartmoor, with a warning as to his future conduct.

It is from this episode that we learn that wine was purchased at a public house by some turnkeys for prisoners in a weak state of health (although Newcombe had never been authorised to do this), and this was probably the Plume of Feathers Inn.

Another turnkey, Mark Wakeham, also found himself in trouble as he was involved in the traffic of straw. His punishment was more severe - instant dismissal. His protests of innocence fell on deaf ears.

In May Major Lee of the militia complained about turnkeys 'harbouring women', while occupiers of some huts were found to be selling spirits. Catel claimed, 'The excessive abuse of strong liquor among the English is generally a dominant passion. They give up everything to satisfy it'.[56] As a consequence of Major Lee's complaint, the Board ordered all the huts to be demolished except those especially allowed by the Board. The inhabitants of those remaining were warned that they would suffer the same fate if they did not behave.

This was not a popular move. Sam Coates wrote to the Board saying he had incurred considerable expense in repairing his hut and asked that it might remain, and that the Board would make him some allowance for it. However, they had no further need for his hut, and claimed that his conduct had been such as to not want any indulgence. This conduct was a violent assault on a prisoner, M. Palafax, and Capt Cotgrave had applied for a warrant for his arrest and subsequent prosecution.

In November, members of the Nottingham Militia had accepted bribes from prisoners in return for being allowed to escape. These prisoners had counterfeited gold coins and forged Bank of England notes. And in December, a forbidden 'straw plait' was found in one of the huts belonging to Mr & Mrs Chapman.

The behaviour of some of the inhabitants of the huts prompted the Board to reassess the situation. As seen above, after the escapade by Mr Wakeham, they decided that all of them were to be taken down. However, it would seem that some of these huts predated the prison. Two of them, sited within the prison boundaries had been in possession of the occupiers for over 40 years. Capt Cotgrave suggested to the Board that their rent should be paid directly to them, but the Board wanted to know by whose authority they occupied them, and to see their leases. It would appear that one of these huts belonged to Mr Edward Carter and his solicitor wrote to the Board saying he had the title deeds to the property.

In the meantime, Mrs Coates, whose husband Sam had been arrested, was attempting to sell her hut to other prison employees. The Board, none too pleased, informed her that this was not to be allowed unless it was understood and settled in writing that no buyer could keep his property in the hut once he was no longer in the employ of the Board.

It was after the straw plait was found in the Chapmans' hut that, on Christmas Eve, the Board issued the following order to Capt Cotgrave:

'...we order you to give immediately a Written Notice to all the Persons occupying the Huts erected within the Prison Boundaries by the Workmen during the Building of the Prison, to quit the same within one month from the Time of your notice when they are all to be pulled down, excepting such as are allowed by our Special Order. The measure has been determined on, according to legal opinion on the subject'.[57] This included Mrs Coates' hut.

Despite these huts being pulled down, prison employees were still given permission to build others or to inclose a piece of land. Richard Jones, the slater and mason was allowed to build a hut for a peppercorn rent.

Outdoor employment of the prisoners was given a trial run. In February, Capt Cotgrave proposed that some should be employed in cutting turf for use in the Prisons and the turnkeys' accommodation. Daniel Alexander recalled this saying, 'the custom was to send the prisoners out to cut the turf in gangs'.[58] They were also permitted to dig the gardens as local labour was impossible to get, and on the understanding that if they tried to escape, this privilege would cease. Repair of the roads was undertaken by prisoners at 6d a day, and in April the contractors were ordered to have wagons with wide wheels.

The Board also had the idea of employing prisoners to make their own 'List' shoes (made from strips of material). Capt Cotgrave said this could not possibly be undertaken unless he had a detached place for them to work in and a proper storehouse. The Board disagreed and said if he could not manage to arrange it as easily as it had been done at Forton Prison near Portsmouth, then a clerk would be employed to do it for him! They expressed annoyance that shoes had been bought from a steward, Mr Newcombe, for the use of patients discharged from the Hospital. Eventually Capt Cotgrave agreed to the manufacture of List shoes if proper materials were supplied; these were to come from London. Captain James Bowen, a Transport Board Commissioner said that the prisoners 'made shoes for the Government, for themselves, and were paid for it; they had wood and list sent them, and they made the shoes'.[59] William Jordan was, in due course, employed as a shoemaker, overseeing the prisoners work no doubt. A shoe store was situated in the row of buildings behind the surgeon's house. Shoe production was not sufficient to supply all the prisoners needs, and orders for footwear continued throughout the occupation of the War Prison. Tailors were also needed, and John Tozer filled this duty alongside that of turnkey.

The market needed a clerk, but as none of those already employed at the prison could be spared, neighbouring banks were requested to recommend someone who could take up the post at the same salary as the other clerks. This turned out to be John Mitchell who was to inspect and sign bank notes tendered by the prisoners, and who successfully intercepted seven forged bank notes in July. His salary was £80 per annum.

Supplies were keeping many businesses in good trade. During this period:

> Messrs Brock & Co of Plymouth were supplying wine.
> John Kroger of Plymouth was given a contract for victualling the prisoners (beef) from
>   1 March.
> Mr William Smith of Plymouth victualled the sick prisoners until 31 August.
> Messrs Watkins & Brown victualled the Hospital rations.
> Mr Billing supplied straw.
> Messrs Gill & Co of Tavistock supplied coals.
> Messrs Joliffe & Banks near Wandsworth supplied cement.
> Messrs Noble & Hunt replaced Mr Kroger at the end of November.
> John Smith & Son provided sacking for beds.
> Joshua Rowe supplied lamp oil.
> Mr Richard Hall supplied moor stone for building.
> John Miles provided £225 worth of coverlets.

Some of the food supplies were giving cause for concern. The prisoners themselves were permitted to inspect their food. Regulation 14 said that three or five prisoners could 'examine the Provisions furnished by the Contractor for the purpose of giving their Opinion whether the Articles are good...'[60] Unfortunately, as will be seen throughout, these 'Articles' were *not* always good! In January, bad bread was supplied over a period of four days and investigation showed that it was the damp weather that had made it not fit for issue. What was really needed were dry store rooms in which to keep the flour etc. In July, inferior bread was issued to the prisoners but the contractors excuse was that they were given three loaves instead of two so were quite happy! In early December, bad bread was supplied by Joshua Rowe of Torpoint, Cornwall, and he was fined £30 with the threat of a £60 fine should it happen again. Rowe later built himself a storehouse at Princetown, which is now The Railway Inn[61] and he also had what was to become Bolt's shop on the corner.

The weather continued to be a problem. Dr Magrath was directed to keep a Journal (now lost) of the weather recording 'the winds, state of the Barometer and Thermometer etc',[62] and a thermometer was ordered, the London price for one being 10s 6d. At the beginning of January, Major Corbutt requested 10 candles per night for each guard due to 'constant Fogs and Darkness',[63] and lamp oil was in great demand. The labourers in their huts were also feeling the cold and on 1 February sent Capt Cotgrave a petition for coals. The Board seemed reluctant to supply these and asked about the viability of supplying peat instead. But they were told that the labourers had no time to cut turf and should be allowed the same amount of coal as the turnkeys, so the Board agreed to this. Building work also had to be halted occasionally.

It was for this period that Thomson gives a list of prison staff. They comprised:

Captain Cotgrave, R.N. Agent	1 steward	1 plumber
William Dyker, surgeon	1 first clerk	1 carter
William Dickson, assistant surgeon	1 store clerk	1 mason
	1 market clerk	1 slater
1 dispenser	1 extra clerk	1 blacksmith
3 hospital mates	10 turnkeys	1 navigator
1 matron	3 labourers	
1 seamstress	1 foreman of works	

Some accounts recorded for 1810 were:

Joshua Rowe for Birch Brooms	£12 18s 9d
Joseph Price for Hammocks	£156 5s
John Smith & Son for sacking etc for cradles	£132 5s 6d
Gill Rundle & Co for coal etc	£132 6s 4d
Gill Rundle & Co for soap, oil etc	£250 19s 2d
Joshua Rowe for lamp oil	£157 6s

Daniel Alexander's Balance of Account

- of Works to the outgrounds	£283 1s 6d
- Local superintendence	£200
- Travelling charges to Dartmoor	£222 2s
- Measuring Works	£299 7s 6d

1811
More buildings, more clothing, more bad bread - and rats

A nd still the building work continued. Mr Pearse, the senior hospital mate, had his request for a shed adjoining his house approved on 4 January, and the Board also asked for estimates for sheds to the other houses as well. Mr Walters, who must have been staying in lodgings, was to be built a house with a garden on the department's land at the angle of the Plymouth Road on the Barracks side.

A stable was to be built for Mr Hutton, who supplied meat from the slaughterhouse, at an estimated cost of £52 10s, and he would pay a rent of £10 p.a. for it. Mr Newcombe was allowed to inclose a small piece of land for a cow.

In May the Board turned down Mr Bennett's request to build a house and said that no further buildings were to be erected for employees of the prison. However, this resolve did not last long; in August, directions were given for two clerks' houses and six other dwellings for an estimated £1,000. Alterations to existing houses were also made such as fitting out a kitchen in Mr Dyker's house at a cost of £9 2s, and also acquiring a copper boiler for his and Mr Walters' house. The airing ground which was often wet and muddy underfoot was to be paved with stone by the prisoners. For whitewashing the prison, they were to be paid 6d a day.

All this building and repair work was not helped by the sacking of Mr Richard Jones, Foreman of the Masons, for insolence.

It was in June that Capt Cotgrave submitted to the Board the 'Expediency of erecting a separate Prison Building for the Confinement of such Prisoners as are in the habit of selling their Clothing etc in order to prevent them mixing with other Prisoners'[64] (i.e. the 'Romans'). It was agreed that a Board member should visit the prison to assess the situation. Two months later came the decision to build two additional Prison buildings to be erected under the direction of Mr Walters who would use a workforce of prisoners. They were to hold 1,000 men in each, according to Thomson. So, in September, Capt Cotgrave asked for 100 masons or bricklayers to be sent from the ships in Plymouth to assist in this work; he got 95. He also ordered two cart horses, to be 'disposed of' after the building work was completed.

Commissioner Searle had expressed a wish for a blacksmith's shop for the employment of prisoners. When it was completed, John Halfyard was employed

Lintel above the 1811 postern gate, with the inscription HENRI PRISONNIER 1813 JOURNE FRANCAIS. *Elisabeth Stanbrook.*

as master smith with an allowance of 24s per week 'giving him strict instruction as to Industry, and Economy, and cautions against Embezzlement by workmen under him'.[65]

The new guard house that had been required was finished by early August and furnished accordingly, and another postern gate was made in the outer perimeter wall to allow guards direct access to the Barracks. Although made in 1811, the lintel bears the inscription HENRI PRISONNIER 1813 JOURNE FRANCAIS. This was presumably added later. There was still an ongoing list of works to be done: the front of the Agent's and surgeon's houses were to be weather slated; a shop or shed was to be erected for use of the Foreman of the Works; some of the houses were to be newly painted including the two lower rooms of the Agent's house; the Prison passages needed repairing and newly laid with flat moor stone; the privies were to be repaired, and also to be newly laid with flat moor stone; a dirt pit was to be provided for each Prison; the lubber-boarding was to be repaired; and the cook house in the Petty Officers' Prison was to be paved with rough moor stone.

In fact, the cook house was built of wood, and Capt Cotgrave obtained permission to replace it altogether with a stone one at a cost of £50 as prisoners tried to escape from it. The material used for the privy floors was later changed to elm secured by iron gratings to prevent escapes.

The walls separating the Prison were to be lined with thick oak or elm planks and filled with nails, and additional sentry boxes were to be installed. Alterations to the fireplaces and chimney flues, at a cost of £8, in the Hospital wards were to be undertaken. Glass was to be fixed in each side of the wooden sentry boxes - a draught-proof measure no doubt.

Building materials were constantly sought. In June, Richard Hall, provider of moor stone was paid £158 13s 9³/₄d. By Lady Day, Mr Pelling had been paid £1,294 11s 8d for supplies of timber. Timber was needed in such large quantities that Messrs Billing & Co were unable to meet the demand and Capt Cotgrave was compelled to advertise for sealed tenders through the Exeter and Plymouth newspapers.

Mr Nosworthy offered to supply 200 feet of timber and 1,000 feet of ash board, while Messrs Start & Co offered 10,000 feet of elm board. This turned out to be cheaper than wood offered by Mr James Broderick of Plymouth, but Captain Cotgrave was instructed to order 200 feet of oak timber from him and then as much of the ash and elm board offered by the other parties as might be required. However, after the first order from Messrs Nosworthy and Start, the Board then directed Capt Cotgrave to order only from Mr Broderick in future.

In July Tyrwhitt (described as Colonel Tyrwhitt) successfully applied to the Board to employ prisoners to work the moor stone within the prison boundaries - presumably at Herne Hole Quarry - and a few days later, he asked for 20 French prisoners to cultivate the moor under a guard supplied by him. Prisoners were also employed as blacksmiths and, due to the length and severity of their day's work, they were paid 1s a day instead of 6d. In all 122 prisoners were employed as masons and 'navigators' during this period.

Clothing was in continual need for the prisoners and on 15 January, Capt Cotgrave ordered 250 pairs of leather shoes, at which the Board expressed surprise. In September, 4,000 Dutch caps were ordered. It would seem that Newcombe found himself in trouble again when, without permission, he ordered a large quantity of wooden soles from Mr Billing which he made into clogs. This action resulted in his dismissal.

In November 200 pairs of leather shoes were ordered plus 100 pairs of trousers for the 'Italians selected by Major Burke'.[66]

More 'junk' was ordered from Plymouth Dock Yard, for making the clews for hammocks.

A large acreage of land had been enclosed by the Board, and Mr John Watts was given permission to graze his cattle on it for a rent, and on condition that he kept the walls in good condition.

Revd Mason's contract for removing prison 'filth' was causing problems and consideration was given to keeping it for improvement of the prison's own land. But in the end the Board decided to change the contract to payment by the year rather than by the load. This was again put out to tender and, again, Revd Mason provided the highest bid at £32 p.a.

As one might expect, rats had become rampant in the prison and were to continue being a nuisance. In an attempt to deal with the matter, the Board directed Capt Cotgrave to employ a ratcatcher, to be paid 1d a rat.

Despite Joshua Rowe's order of bad bread at the end of 1810, he was allowed to continue supplying the prisoners on the assurance that only good quality food would be provided in future. However, in May, the prisoners rejected both his bread and his beef, much to the surprise of the Board.

From May to September 1810 Rowe had also supplied the prisoners employed as masons with 88 hogsheads of beer. However, in June 1811 he tried telling the Board that he could not supply beer at the price stipulated in their order, but that he could still supply it, he having established a brewery on Dartmoor (at Bachelors Hall). But they insisted common beer of the country should be supplied and a 1d profit per gallon allowed. The following month Rowe claimed he was unable to supply codfish beyond the ensuing week and would like to substitute it with white herring. Somewhat annoyed the Board refused, saying that other contractors managed to supply it and that he should have got in better stocks. By the end of July Rowe had been given notice to quit on 31 October, due to a continuing supply of bad bread and no vegetables. Back at Torpoint, Mr Rowe claimed that no cabbage or turnips could be got in sufficient quantities for supplying the prisoners. As a result he had caused large quantities to be planted, and hoped that he might keep his contract. But his excuse was to no avail, and he remained sacked.

The prisoners themselves continued to be a nuisance. In early June A. Ricard deliberately broke eight lamps and was handcuffed and placed, during daytime, in the middle of the market place.

It was towards the end of 1811 that the Board asked about the progress of the building of a church. Capt Cotgrave had to admit that, although one had been planned, it had not yet been started (see below pp 77-84).

1812
Fire at the bakehouse, 'scandalous bread', endless building work and Turnpike Trust tolls

S now was a major cause of concern at the start of 1812. Capt Cotgrave requested that supplies of bread and beef could be kept at the prison in case they became cut off, and that snow be melted for drinking water rather than running a water course from a spring near his house to the prison. The Board themselves ordered that cattle for consumption by the prisoners should be killed at the prison's slaughterhouse.

Repairs and alterations continued apace. In February, three doors on the Military Way were lined with elm and nailed to prevent them being cut through by prisoners. Some of the Barrack buildings also needed repairs. The following month, sixty worn out locks on the prison doors and gates were in need of repair, and an extension to the slaughterhouse was authorised at a cost of £12 15s. May saw the prison being whitewashed and prisoners used to make Capt Cotgrave a gate for a small inclosure near his house. In June, prisoners were employed for repairing the prison boundary and for cutting turf. Four new boilers were ordered for the general cook house.

The new Prisons, smaller in size than the others and apparently 10 bays long,[68] were unfinished still and the Board asked Capt Cotgrave when they would be ready. By June Capt Cotgrave was having to wait a month for the necessary scaffolding to arrive. But Mr Walters, in July, said that they would be in a fit state to receive prisoners by October. In fact he said that they could house up to two hundred prisoners immediately, perhaps comprising fifty Petty Officers as their own Prison was so crowded. In September Mr Walters suggested that iron bars and shutters should be fixed in the windows of the upper galleries. The oak plank floors in these Prisons made them more popular than the other five, although one of them (No.2) had a stone ground floor.

Further works ordered in late October included a shed to be erected for wagons and carts

belonging to the department with a straw loft over, at an estimate of £200; a roof to be put on the current coal shed, at an estimate of £7; a small shed to be erected to shelter prisoners offering their authorised 'manufactures' for sale, at an estimate of £2; prison lamps were to be

All that survives of the newer Prison No.6; it was much reduced in height in the 1940s.
© *Crown copyright NMR.*

covered in wire to stop prisoners breaking them; windows were to be made in each of the guard rooms towards the Military Way; a partition was to be made in the kitchen of the surgeon's house, and both this and the passage was also to be floored at an estimate of £15 10s. Repairs to the slaughterhouse costing £1 17s 6d were also carried out. In the meantime, Mr Broderick had sent a bill to the Board for £2,269 15s 9d for timber used in the building of the Prisons.

Messrs Hoine & Stackhouse of Liverpool supplied sheet lead for the prison for 6 months, while Messrs Billing & Co were paid £1,055 16s 6d for their timber and other unspecified articles.

Carts were being built by the prisoners to assist in the moving of materials for building work, and in August, a wagon to carry hay for the horses belonging to the Board was to be built at a cost of £20.

Prisoners were being employed by outside bodies. In July, five months after the Act discussed above, the Dartmoor and Roborough Turnpike Trustees applied to the Board to employ 20 French prisoners attended by a guard from the Barracks to work on the building of this road in the vicinity of the prison in return for wages.

The iron railway was still causing interest from would-be buyers. Mr W. Chonine of Plymouth made enquiries about it in June. But it was not for sale. In fact, later in the year, it was decided to spend money on another wrought iron railway for the prison instead of lubber boarding for the new Prisons.

A fire in Mr Richard Fillis' and Mr Martin Thomas' (formerly Mr Cooper's) bakehouse in Two Bridges Road on 8 October made the Board review their fire control capabilities. It was extinguished by the prison's fire engine but it was suggested that the Barracks should have their own engine - which would have been nearer. This was ordered by the Barrack Board shortly after the fire, but the Transport Board said it had to go in the prison engine-house for the present! Capt Cotgrave also requested that two wells should be sunk to prevent the scarcity of water in case of future fires and severe frosts. This cost £10. Two dozen leather fire buckets were also ordered. The cost of these, obtained from Plymouth, was not given, but in London the price of one dozen 3-gallon fire buckets was £6 16s 6d.

The bakehouse was rebuilt by a team of prisoners comprising 12 masons, 6 labourers and 6 carpenters.

Mr Mason's agreement for the disposal of the prison soil was due to expire on 31 July. The Board felt that the agreement should not be renewed as the dung could be used for the general cultivation of the ground within the prison boundaries.

Escapes were still being attempted or made. Perhaps the most famous one took place in August, when Capt Cotgrave had to report that Louis Francois Vanhille had escaped on 22 August, to London he assumed, and that other prisoners had attempted to escape from the Petty Officers' Prison but had got caught. These were confined to the Cachot and not released until October. The sentinel on duty had been promised £40 to help them escape and had received £3 in part. However, he returned this to Major Bigland who suggested he kept it 'for having so faithfully discharged his Duty'.[69]

The escape by Vanhille has been well covered in many other publications and a full account can be found in Thomson (pp.35-44). Suffice to say that his escape was aided by a brewer from

Launceston and his two daughters, Mary Ellis (a market trader from Tavistock), and one or two others with whom he had forged a bond when on parole in Launceston. It was Mary Ellis who smuggled into the market a set of wagoners clothes into which Vanhille surreptitiously changed and then left the market with the other traders at the close of day. He spent his initial months of freedom wandering from town to town throughout the country and eventually boarded a ship at Bristol, bound for Jamaica, under the name of Mr Williams. He aroused suspicion and, upon investigation, his true identity was revealed. Thus he found himself once more a prisoner of war.

In September, two prisoners escaped from a working party. As the buildings were nearly finished, a stronger guard was placed over them and, at the end of October, two more prisoners were apprehended as they tried to escape from 'procuring stone for the New Buildings at Dartmoor'.[71] December saw thirty-seven prisoners confined in the Cachot with short allowances, for buying bedding and hammocks belonging to other prisoners.

Quality of food supplies was still giving cause for concern. In February, a sample of meal sent to Dartmoor's bakehouse by Mr Fillis (his 'flour' came from Plymouth) was bad, the Board informing him that 'you will be severely mulcted for your very extraordinary and unprecedented Conduct'.[72] A letter written a week later revealed that this meal was ground rice! Mr William Cock of Plymouth Dock, who victualled the prisoners in health from March, was also fined for bad bread during this period.

It would seem that Mr Cock was not unduly worried by his fine as he continued to supply inferior food to the prisoners. In late July they rejected his supply of fish, and in August he issued 1,992 lbs of cod and 7,255 lbs of potatoes short of the necessary rations. For this he was heavily fined, and Capt Cotgrave had to bring in a supply of biscuit in case of a reoccurrence.

After the bakehouse burnt down, supplies of bread became difficult for a while. The prisoner's ration, baked in the Board's ovens, was cut from 1½ lbs to 1lb, and the deficiency was made up with biscuits as the contractor would not use Mr Hagerman's bakehouse facilities offered to him free of charge. But the prisoners refused this and became riotous. So hungry were some of the 'Romans' that they scavenged for scraps in the rubbish heaps. On this occasion, when the two-horse cart came to collect the rubbish, the 'Romans' set upon the horses, killing them with homemade implements, and eating the warm flesh.

Matters did not get better and the contractor started supplying 'scandalous bread',[72] which meant that even more biscuit had to be bought, while the contractor was given a warning to improve the quality of supplies.

The fish supplied by Mr Cock was rejected by the prisoners again in September. He was ordered to send a sample to the Board, which was of good quality, and they questioned Capt Cotgrave's accusation that it was bad. He was not amused, which is reflected in his letter sent to Mr Cock a few days later complaining of his 'very shameful conduct, and particularly sending a very fine Cod-fish to the Board, as a fair Sample of what you were serving to the Prisoners at Dartmoor and had been objected to...'[73] He was threatened with the termination of his contract should he misbehave again. Nevertheless, in October, he was allowed an advance of £12,000 on his contract for victualling at the prison and, towards the end of the month, he was given permission to employ prisoners 'to erect additional Ovens on the Moor'.[74] He then started supplying the prison with bread at a very late hour of the day, and he was fined £100.

The sale of 'small beer' seemed to be a profitable enterprise. In early November, several employees were given a share (of the profits) from these sales:

Robert Holmden, a clerk	£50
J. Bennett, store clerk	£45
J. Mitchell, market clerk	£40
N. Bennett, extra clerk	£35
J. Knapman, canteen clerk	£35
J. Arnold, steward	£30
T. Dyer, hospital steward	£30

Supplies for the prisoners were still being bought in bulk. 4,000 beds were shipped on board the transport at Portsmouth in June, and in July 1,000 pairs of shoes were ordered. 5,000 washed blankets and 2,000 beds were forwarded from Plymouth to Dartmoor in September. In November, at a cost of £12, Capt Cotgrave bought a covering for the Board's wagon used in transporting the invalid prisoners to Plymouth.

Messrs Cauldrey & Son of White Cross Street, Cripplegate obtained a contract for lighting the prison lamps at the end of October but were told to reduce their terms. They planned to send someone to Dartmoor to survey the lamps but were told that the prospective lamplighter could not be allowed a place to sleep at the prison.

The Dartmoor and Roborough Turnpike Trust placed an advertisement in the *Exeter Flying Post* on 19 November, for the auctioning of six months worth of tolls arising from the toll gate 'called Prince Town Gate' (i.e. the one near the Plume of Feathers Inn) and Rundle Stone Gate. The auction took place at the Duchy Hotel on Wednesday 15 December. A glimpse of what a bidder might expect to receive, based on previous income, was also published:

Sums Collected at Gates

Prince Town Gate	19 August - 13 November incl.	£80 13s 8d
Rundle Stone Gate	14 September - 13 November incl	£10 14s 8d

By November 1812 the number of prisoners at Dartmoor was about 9,000.[75] Space was cramped, despite the new buildings, but it was cramped for the militia too. At the end of December, Capt Cotgrave was instructed to remove all prisoners from the Petty Officers' Prison to make way for additional accommodation needed for the guards. The prisoners were to be sent to the upper storey of one of the new prisons as soon as possible.

Towards the end of 1812 Mr John Wethams made a detailed drawing of the prison complex together with a key to most of the buildings to date. This formed the frontispiece of Thomson's book and, although rather fanciful in certain aspects, it is useful in that, by now, most of the main buildings had been erected. A wall extended across the prison complex dividing the seven Prisons from the civil buildings. Between the Hospital and the Petty Officers' Prison was the market square.

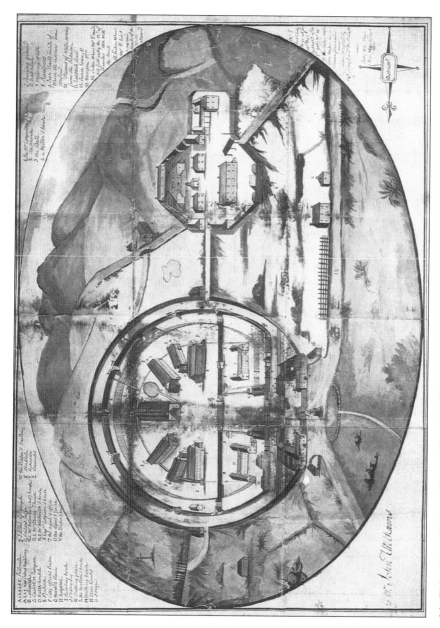

John Wethams' plan of Dartmoor Prison and Barracks in 1812. Mr Carpenter's House stands next to the small bakehouse on the lower right. *Frontispiece from Thomson's book.*

What cannot be seen on any of the plans or maps are the arches and piers built into the ground floors of the Hospital and Petty Officers' Prison. These were made necessary by the uneven ground on which they were built.

The Prisons on Wethams' plan were numbered 1 to 5 in a semi-circle, with the new No.6 between 1 and 2, and No.7 between 4 and 5. Other plans of the period show that they were numbered consecutively in the semi circle. Each had its own macadamised yard. The Cachot was between the inner boundary wall and the iron railing fence, to the north of Prison No.1. Interestingly, Wethams did not draw in the airing sheds that appear in other contemporary drawings and the East guard house appears not to have been built.

The Barracks were reached via a walkway from the southern end of the Military Way. The dead house (mortuary) was outside the complex to the north, as was the burying ground, sometimes known as 'dead man's land', both reached via three gates, one in each wall and fence.

Wethams' plan also showed the water courses inside the prison. Water was brought to the prison in a leat taken off the R. Walkham, supplemented by the Spriddle Lake, to a reservoir opposite the prison gate on the opposite side of the road. The take-off point is interesting as good quality masonry survives on the weir. Alexander's own description of his design of water courses from the reservoir is as follows: 'and is then divided into five different channels, with sluices to regulate the quantity of each: two of those channels diverge to the right, and two to the left; they are conducted through the foul sewers of the prison, and the middle channel is preserved entirely separate, and forms the conduit for clean water to every part of the prison, and those are so formed as that the whole quantity might be sent down any channel, or distributed in the five channels at pleasure'.[76] From No.4, they discharged through a grating under the boundary wall and into the foul leat. The channels passing through the privies measured, according to Catel, 6 feet in width and 2 feet in depth. An oval bathing pond between Prisons 3 and 4 was filled if the weather was warm enough for bathing. There was another pool in the yard of the Petty Officers' Prison, fed by an open water course. Some prisoners, wanting to earn a few pennies, washed clothes in the section of the water courses that had passed through the kitchens. The water was deemed clean enough for such purposes! Dipping wells in other parts of the prison complex, not shown on the plan, helped augment supplies. Piped water was also taken from the reservoir to the Barracks.

Wetham's plan erroneously shows Bachelor's Hall corn mill by Trena or Ockery Bridge, together with a house which may be the now demolished Ockery Cottage. This latter building might have been lived in by a miller, but Thomson's statement that a mill existed at Trena Bridge, based on Wethams' plan, is misleading.[77]

Detail of the arches in the Hospital wall.
Elisabeth Stanbrook.

The reservoir opposite the entrance to the Prison.
Elisabeth Stanbrook.

The prison leat take-off point; the R. Walkham does a
sharp bend to the right.
Elisabeth Stanbrook.

Also shown on the plan is 'Mr Carpenter's House', (he later owned the slaughterhouse) now surviving as Isca, and one of the bakeries; this possibly survives as an outbuilding in the grounds of Hisworthy House. Both are on the Tavistock Road.[78]

Some payments recorded for 1812 are:

Mr J. Webber	£61	4s
Messrs Gill & Co	£53	14s 8d
Messrs Gill & Co	£240	13s
Mr T. Husband	£226	17s
Mr T. Husband	£79	12s
Mrs Mary Rowe	£105	17s 2d

Reference is also made to the turnkey's salary which was £50 p.a.[79]

1813
Americans versus French, segregation work, Turnpike Trust trouble, goodbye Capt Cotgrave

From time to time, employees of the Board received call-up papers. In January, Mr William May, a mason and slater, informed the Board he had been told to serve in the local militia, and requested the Board's protection. But they said it was not in their powers to relieve him but that he could stay in his situation during the time he was serving.

Reception of the new troops in the Petty Officers' Prison required some modifications to be made which were carried out in early January. They included fixing cross rails against the hammock posts for slinging the hammocks, and the preparation of tables and forms. The arm racks were not permitted until after the troops were installed.

The troops had to be supplied with bedding, and Capt Cotgrave's order for this provoked an outcry from the Board. He had supplied them with:

49	iron bradles
49	sackings [tackings?]
829	beds
848	blankets
434	rugs
469	palliasses
331	hammocks
993	clews

The Board demanded to know how many troops there were and how the above articles were to be distributed. They had never heard of a soldier having two beds and more than one palliasse for each hammock! Capt Cotgrave sent a rather defensive reply stating that some soldiers were married and therefore allowed a double quantity of bedding. Also, Major Cotton had applied for more bedding due to the severity of the weather, saying they should have a blanket put under and a rug and blanket put over them to enable them to keep warm. He then revealed that the total number of non-commissioned officers and privates doing duty at the Prison was 789.

The Board was not happy saying that items were still in excess of requirements. They worked out that there was an excess of 69 beds, 89 blankets, 54 rugs and 469 palliasses and demanded a further explanation. They also demanded that 331 clews be withdrawn as only two per hammock were allowed. In the end, they permitted extra supplies to remain at Dartmoor rather than being sent back.

Dartmoor Prison in October 1813, as sketched by Captain Durrant of the militia on duty at that time.
Hampshire County Council Museums Service.

Removal of the Petty Officers from their prison to that of the new one where ordinary prisoners were confined proved to be problematic. On 5 January, Capt Cotgrave reported that on starting to remove some of the Petty Officers into the two upper floors of one of the new Prisons, a considerable number of the 'common prisoners' had rushed in amongst them and 'committed many depredations' by cutting down their hammocks and robbing others. Four ringleaders were caught and confined in the Cachot on two thirds rations until early February. As a result, two bulkheads were fixed at the top of the steps separating the Petty Officers from the other prisoners. These prisoners still caused annoyance and, a day later, the Petty Officers requested successfully that others of 'bad character' were also put in the Cachot.

The Cachot appears to have been rather full in January as Capt Cotgrave obtained permission to send 16 of the prisoners confined within it to Plymouth to prevent disease and overcrowding. In May it came to his attention that tools were being smuggled into the Cachot through the railing from prisoners in the great prison yard who were burying them in the ground undiscovered by the sentinels. He requested that a small doorway be created in the Military Way opposite the Cachot, which would prevent this. On agreeing to this, those prisoners inside the Cachot were removed to the guard house and handcuffed until they could be returned again.

General supplies for prisoners continued. In January, Capt Cotgrave received a clothes supply of:

2,000 Dutch caps
5,000 jackets
5,000 waistcoats
5,000 pairs trousers
5,000 shirts

The following June he ordered 2,000 pairs of leather shoes and 2,000 pairs of stockings for prisoners to march in. In addition, he ordered:

5,000 caps
5,000 jackets
5,000 waistcoats
5,000 pairs trousers
5,000 shirts

It hardly needs to be said that building work continued! Staff houses were still in need of attention. In mid-February John Moore, an interpreter, requested that an iron pot be placed on his chimney to prevent smoking. Capt Cotgrave took this opportunity to voice similar complaints he had had from other staff, resulting in the order given for all such houses to be fitted with iron pots.

The walls of Prison No.4 (formerly No.3) were undergoing repair due to damage by prisoners, and on their completion the 'Romans' were to be confined here. In April 1,400 prisoners were moved into the building on short allowance as a punishment for the damage. They were supplied with brown cotton shirts with yellow sleeves to try and stop them disposing of them.

Mr Walters sent the Board a letter about the decayed state of the floors in Prison No.5, especially the third floor, in February. He recommended that they be laid with 2 inch oak planks. The Board were not happy with this and asked whether they could not be laid with moor stone as they had been in Plymouth's new prison. But Mr Walters explained that this would be a third more expensive, so they suggested that the plank floors could be coated with plate iron in bands 1½ inches broad and laid 3 inches apart, and securely fixed to the floor. However, as Mr Walters pointed out to them, prisoners could arm themselves with these bands and attempt escapes. The Board had to see the sense of this and instructed him to do nothing with the floors for the time being!

The airing sheds that had eventually been erected were, by now, considered to be useless due to the inclemency of the weather and, on this basis, Plymouth was not permitted to have any either!

Other houses needed weather slating. In June Mr Moore asked for a turf house for his house. This was approved by the Board so long as it did not exceed £10 to build and that he maintained it himself. In July it was decided that the turnkey and the labourers houses could be divided without affecting the buildings for the sum of £2 for each house. In October they were given permission to build sheds at the backs of their houses to protect them from the inclement weather. This was allowed at a cost of £5.

Fire broke out at the slaughterhouse in July. The roof had comprised thatch and was consequently totally destroyed. It was decided to repair the roof with slates.

Decay seemed a regular occurrence in the Prisons. In September it was reported that the passages in the five older prisons were in a decayed state and that 12,000 feet of planks of oak 2 inches thick should be laid; this was not ordered until mid-November, with instructions that Capt Cotgrave should seek the 'best terms in his Power'. Further damage by the 'Roman' prisoners was also caused to 280 lubber boards in Prison No.4 and had to be repaired at a cost of £20.

Privy No.7, covered with Portland stone, had by December been stripped of all its 100 feet of copper fastenings and some of the stone itself. Consideration as to whether the privy should be slated was turned down by the Board who said that as the prisoners had brought the problem on themselves, they could live with it.

Messrs Cauldrey & Son, the lamplighters were causing problems as they could not meet the order of lamp oil, and Capt Cotgrave had had to order it from Plymouth.

The shrubs in the plantation on the northern side of the prison were by now quite dead. Capt Cotgrave managed to get permission to remove them and convert the land into a grass field.

Prisoners were still being employed by Sir Thomas Tyrwhitt and Revd Mason but Capt Cotgrave got wind of an escape plan in May and put a stop to this. However the Board overruled him and said the work was to continue, using only those prisoners who were unlikely to try and escape. Only if such an incident occurred were the working parties to stop. In August Joshua Rowe applied to the Board to use French prisoners in making improvements to his land at Bachelors Hall and assured them that he would be responsible for their safe return to the prison. However, the Board refused this request.

Arrival of the Americans

On 25 March, with the American War well underway the order had been given that 250 American prisoners at Plymouth should be sent to Dartmoor. The extra prisoners prompted the ordering of six new sentry boxes and, in April, the new East guard room was made ready for occupation.

The 250 prisoners came from various parts of America including Boston, Maine, Marblehead, New York, Portland and Virginia. On 3 April, the prisoners set off on foot at 10.30am and, after only one stop, arrived at the prison later in the day. Their first impression was not favourable. Charles Andrews, who was among the prisoners, records that snow lay on the ground, and in the vicinity of the prison, were 'miserable cottages' in which labourers selling turf lived. Inside, each American 'cast his hapless eyes around the prison, he saw the water constantly dropping from the cold stone walls on every side, which kept the floor (made of stone) constantly wet, and cold as ice'.[80] On 1 May, Capt Cotgrave ordered that all American prisoners be put into Prison No.4 with the Romans.

This was not a good move! Relations between the Americans and the 'Romans' did not run smoothly and eventually degenerated into a serious brawl when, in July, the Americans found themselves ambushed in the yard where they were attacked by the 'Romans' armed with stones and clubs. Guards intervened and all recovered from their injuries. But, on 20 July, Capt Cotgrave reported that this serious quarrel between the two parties necessitated the building of a high wall to divide the already enclosed yard into two at a cost of £70. At the end of the month, he had also ordered a new cooker to be made so that they could cook separately from each other too. The whole incident was serious enough to warrant an Inquiry, conducted by Lieut-General Stephens, the Commander of the Plymouth Garrison, and Mr Hawker, a Plymouth magistrate who were so disgusted at how the 'Romans' were living that they ordered their removal to the Plymouth hulks. On 21 August Capt Cotgrave received orders to remove 200 at once, with the rest to follow. They would be replaced by other prisoners from Plymouth.[81] On 23 October, the Board approved the moving of the black and coloured American prisoners to the Prisons inhabited by the French (for reasons not specified). Later on, the American equivalent of the 'Romans' were the 'Rough Alleys' who, although unsocial and filthy, did not sink to the depths of the French.

Mr Reuben G. Beasley was the Agent for American prisoners of war. He appears to have been indifferent to their plight of receiving no income from the USA Government with which to buy market produce to supplement their meagre rations. On 23 April the 250 American prisoners requested soap and tobacco which they claimed the British prisoners of war were getting from the USA government. The Board said if they could prove it, they could have them. However, it was not until January 1814 that funds for soap and tobacco were forthcoming.

For 4 July some American prisoners hoisted American colours in the Prison and behaved in a 'riotous manner'. The military soon had them under control and one American was put in the Cachot.

Bank note forgeries by prisoners were not uncommon. An interesting example is the case of prisoner D'Orange who, in the records, is revealed as one of the merchants who sold bone work for his fellow prisoners. By 14 November, D'Orange had been in the Cachot for forgery for eight days and Capt Cotgrave asked that he might be released because he was claiming ignorance of this crime and, that as seller of bone work, he was needed by his fellow prisoners. The Board approved his release two days later, but overturned their decision on 20 November because, in the meantime, Capt Cotgrave had acquired some new information. A letter had been handed over to him by a Capt Bautranche containing remarks about people forging and dealing in bank notes, and it appeared that D'Orange was a principle dealer 'in this illicit traffic'.[82] So his incarceration in the Cachot continued. Charles Andrews claimed that, in all, bank notes were forged to the value of £150,000, and many of these were copies of notes belonging to the Plymouth Commercial Bank, the Tamar Bank and the Launceston and Totnes Bank. Silver coins were also forged using Spanish dollars brought in from outside. From 1 dollar they could make 8 English shillings.

Illness amongst prisoners continued to be a problem. In March, a measles epidemic broke out. The Hospital ward No.2 was cleaned and prepared for those with it to prevent further contagion. Towards the end of April Capt Cotgrave told the Board that many French prisoners had died because they sold their clothes and bedding, referring to it as 'an inhuman practice'. In May two prisoners were wounded when they blew up rocks for stone. They were to be sent to France with other invalids. Other records show that injuries from rock blasting were not uncommon. 'We had a great many accidents from the men being employed in blasting rocks; we had a great many wounded in that duty'.[83]

Smallpox broke out in Princetown during September and all Sir Thomas Tyrwhitt's working parties were stopped together with those working for the Turnpike Trust. Mr Dyker the surgeon was permitted to send to Plymouth's Royal Hospital for a vaccine. By 10 October, six American prisoners were confined in the Hospital.

The amount of food needed to victual thousands of men meant that surrounding farms were able to prosper at this time. From Brown's House, a remote farmstead north of Postbridge, came dairy produce. Sale particulars for Gidleigh Barton in 1813 state that the premises were within 10 miles 'of the New Prison at Dartmoor, where the Produce of the Estate may be disposed of to great Advantage'. Hemery cites William Reep of Nattor Farm near Mary Tavy, who delivered dairy produce by packhorse to the prison Hospital. In January 1814, as well as quantities of butter, he delivered 258 gallons and 2 quarts of milk at $10^1/_2$d a gallon, and 16 gallons and 2 quarts at 16d a gallon.

Carriers were also kept busy delivering goods; for example, Mr Bond of Plymouth was listed as a carrier to Dartmoor Prison in a local directory of 1814.[84]

Bad quality food continued as usual with many complaints from the prisoners over the months. Mr Cock's fish was again rejected by the prisoners in late January. In June contractor Mr Billing had been trying to supply very inferior produce. Bread issued on 14 June was condemned and returned for other bread in lieu. The Scotch barley was also condemned. As a result, Mr Bennett had to be sent into Tavistock the evening before to purchase whatever he could get such as rice, pease or barley in order that the prisoners would not go without. In July Billing was again fined for bad food, so it is not surprising therefore that he was informed that his contract would cease on 30 September. Bad bread remained in constant supply. In August Capt Cotgrave acquired samples of bread and meal from the store and bakehouse in Tavistock Road and sent them to the

Board's Inspector. They ordered that samples be sent to Mr Magan the baker and to ask him of what they consist. The controversy continued and Messrs Bawden and Fox of Princetown were employed by the Board as informers to search the stores of the bread contractor. They found 100 to 150 sacks of barley meal which had consistently been used instead of wheat. This saga had ongoing and serious consequences which are recorded in Appendix II. Needless to say, Hagerman, Drake and Twynham's services were no longer acceptable, and Gill & Co (sometimes referred to as Gill & Hornbrook) from Tavistock took over the bakehouse. Complaints were also received about the small beer with requests that it be obtained from another supplier, to which the Board had no objection.

Revd Mason also tried to supply the prison with potatoes; his bill for £50 was not allowed by the Board.

It was Mr Bennett who owned Prince Town Brewery (behind the Duchy Hotel) and was supplying the prisoners with 'table beer'. In February he sent the Board a copy of an Excise Warrant directing that the price of small beer should be increased from 20s to 24s per barrel. As he had served the prisoners at 18s per barrel, he requested that he might increase this to 24s. But the Board would only agree to 22s.

In February, regardless of the complaints, small beer shares were awarded to:

Mr R. Holmden, first clerk	£20
J. Bennett, store clerk	17s
J. Mitchell, market clerk	13s
W. Bennett, extra clerk	13s
J. Moore, extra clerk	13s
J. Knapman, canteen clerk	13s
J. Arnold, steward clerk	13s
T. Dyer, hospital clerk	13s
Mr Walters	13s

Another supplier of beer was the Tamar Brewery near Plymouth Dock. One of the partners was Martin Thomas who co-leased the bakehouse on the Two Bridges Road with Mr Fillis.

With so many American and French prisoners needing accommodation by September, the Board asked Capt Cotgrave if the Petty Officers' Prison could be vacated by the military to make room for them. The reply was yes, and that 650 prisoners could be housed there. But if no further American prisoners were sent to the prison, there would be room for 1,300 French prisoners! So Capt Cotgrave was authorised to contact the Commanding Officer with the plan. This was not well received, and Major Searle said that the Garrison was too full of military personnel to accommodate those in the Petty Officers' Prison. So this plan was shelved. A month later the Barrack Master had given orders for the iron bars in the windows to be removed and replaced with sash windows, further indicating their determination to stay put. None too pleased, the Board reminded them that the building was part of the prison and had only been lent to them temporarily; therefore they were to put the windows back as they found them when they vacated the building.

The Turnpike Trust was the cause of some annoyance to the Board. In mid July, the road within the prison boundary was in need of repairs. As there was a turnpike gate at each entrance to the prison boundary, a toll had to be paid each time anyone went in or out. Capt Cotgrave felt that the road should therefore be repaired by the Turnpike Trust but they disagreed. The Board, in turn, responded by saying that if the road was part of the public highway for which tolls were being paid, then the trustees must pay for the repairs. If this is was not to be the case, then their own large gates were to be erected so that no one except those with business at the prison would be allowed entry. It is not recorded how this dispute was settled. However, an advertisement in the *Exeter Flying Post* on 29 July revealed that the Dartmoor and Roborough Turnpike Trust was in financial difficulty. They wanted:

'to BORROW, on the credit of the TOLLS... the sum of FOUR HUNDRED POUNDS, in any sums not less than Fifty Pounds, which will be secured by deeds poll (to be delivered free of expense) bearing interest at 5*l* per cent per annum, *clear of the property-tax*'.

On 3 November Capt Cotgrave forwarded a letter to the Board from a Capt Bell who advised that he was to supersede him as Agent at Dartmoor. Thinking that his departure was imminent, Capt Cotgrave requested the use of wagons and horses to remove his belongings from the prison. But he was told it was very unlikely that Bell would take up the post and was advised to stay put; by 11 November confirmation of this had reached Capt Cotgrave.

By 15 November Viscount Melville of the Admiralty announced that, despite a recommendation to stay, Capt Cotgrave was indeed to be removed from Dartmoor in accordance with the ruling that such appointments expired every three years. Captain Thomas Shortland was to take over. On 22 November Capt Cotgrave confirmed receipt of the Board's instructions to hand over to Capt Shortland all the prisoners and stores at Dartmoor, which he did the following day. He was permitted to use a wagon to transport his goods from the prison.

Capt Shortland, by all accounts a more lenient man than his predecessor, wasted no time in demanding repairs to Capt Cotgrave's former house, complete with estimate. But this demand was turned down and he was told to wait until spring. However he was given permission to use the former bedroom as an office and to fit it out with shelves. Undeterred, he then asked that the footway outside his and the surgeon's house be raised, and this was allowed. In December, he further asked to erect a stable by using old materials of a temporary shed in the Agent's square for his horse, and this was also permitted.

Having settled in, Capt Shortland visited all the Prison buildings and reported back to the Board his findings that the ground floors were very worn with holes. However, he had also found a reference in a letter from the Board to an order of 5 August 1811 directing that the prison passages were to be laid with flat moor stone, and he asked them what he should do. They replied that he should investigate why this order had not been carried out by questioning Mr Walters or Capt Cotgrave.

Upon questioning, Mr Walters acknowledged that the ground floors of the Prisons should have been paved with the moor stone but could give no reason why this had not yet been done. He was consequently ordered to attend to the floors in Prison No.4 and of the privies 'at once' and then to do the others.

Towards the end of November Messrs Isbell, Rowe & Co approached the Board saying they had sustained losses under the contract for building Dartmoor Prison, and could they be remunerated for these. But it would appear that the Board had already given them a 'considerable' extra allowance and they could have no more.

The Revd J.P. Jones of North Bovey made an excursion over the moor to Princetown during 1813, which he recorded in a pamphlet he published in 1823. His opinion was favourable, and his admiration for the complex was evident; 'several large buildings of an oblong form, 300 feet in length, and 50 feet in breadth... well aired, abundantly supplied with excellent water, and the enclosed courts were spacious'.[85]

Jones then went on to give a description of what he saw when he mounted a wall in the outer court:

'...the unfortunate men were amusing themselves in the best manner they were able; their hammocks were hung out to be aired, and in general they appeared but little affected with their truly pitiable situation'.

He also observed working parties:

'Many were permitted to leave the Prison and work on the moor; we passed several parties consisting of about 10 or 12; they were employed in blowing up the rocks and improving the soil; care was taken to select those least acquainted with the English language'.[86]

The winter weather was still taking its toll on the welfare of prison staff and the Board recommended that sentry boxes with glass panes be placed at the lower gates of the prison to shelter the turnkeys.

Some bills recorded for 1813 were:

January:

Mr Hagerman (for biscuits) £54 13s 6d

August:

Messrs Gill, Rundle & Co	-	Coals	£244	11s	6d
Messrs Gill, Rundle & Co	-	Lime	£189	8s	1d
Mrs Mary Rowe	-	Slate	£298	8s	9d
Mr J. Webber	-	Bricks	£89	5s	

December:

Messrs Gill Rundle & Co	Coals	£344	14s	2d
Mrs Mary Rowe	Slate	£454	14s	
Messrs Gill, Rundle & Co	Lime	£203	1s	9d
Mr J. Webber	Bricks	£187	7s	4d

1814
Snow cuts off Prison, swarms of rats, 'creeping friends' and ongoing disrepair

Freezing weather marked the start of 1814. According to Hoskins, the snowfall in the south west was the greatest in living memory, and that nationally the frosts lasted until 20 March. The depth of snow that fell in Princetown in January was such that drifts in the yards were as high as the walls. The 'buckets in the prison, in the short space of four hours, froze ten or twelve quarts to a solid'.[87] The Plymouth road was blocked, cutting off supplies, and the emergency rations in the storehouse were also unreachable. So Capt Shortland supplied 80 prisoners to be employed by the Dartmoor and Roborough Turnpike Trust for the purpose of clearing the turnpike road of snow and, a few days later, this number had risen to 100. Others were employed in clearing a way through to the storehouse.

It was on the night of 19/20 January that eight American prisoners tried to escape by making a hole in a wall into an outside privy and scaling a wall, but only one succeeded, the others being caught. The escapee was eventually defeated by the weather and sought sanctuary at a moorman's hut and was subsequently turned in. The culprits were confined in the Cachot.

The weather in January was so severe that Capt Shortland allowed the contractor to supply 'a proper proportion of pearl barley'[88] in lieu of vegetables which could not be obtained. He also had to order salt beef and biscuits in lieu of fresh, and order lamp oil from Tavistock instead of Plymouth as the roads were impassable due to the snow.

By the end of February, the road had been badly damaged and complaints were made by 'the Waggoner & Navigator of this Department'.[89] Capt Shortland obtained permission to have this road repaired on occasions by the Department 'should it be injured by their Carts but not to take the charge of repairs always of it'.[90]

American prisoners arriving at Dartmoor Prison at the end of January experienced this appalling weather. Perez Drinkwater, some of whose letters back home survive, had been captured during the last few days of 1813, was landed at Plymouth on 20 January 1814, transferred to a prison ship the *Brave* on 24 January, was landed from her on 31 January and marched to Dartmoor 'in a snowstorm'. His letters [punctuation and spelling are his] are poignant, with an underlying sense of anger and despair:

> '... it either snows or rains the whole year round and is cold enough to wear a great coat the whole time... This is the first time that I was ever deprived of my Liberty and when I sit and think of it almost deprives me of my sences for we have nothing else to do but sit and reflect on our preasant situation which is bad enough god noes for we have but 1lb and a half of black bread and about 3 ounces of beef and a Little beef tee to drink and all that makes us one meal a Day the rest of the time we have to fast which is hard times for the days are very Long heir now I want to get out of heir before the war is over so that I can have the pleasure of killing one Englishman and drinking his blood which I think I could do with a good will

for I think them the worst of all the human race for their is no crimes but what they are gilty of...'.

At last, January saw the USA Government provide each prisoner with 1¹/₂d a day to buy tobacco or potatoes and soap. Nathaniel Pierce, whose diary also survived, received 4s 9d as wages due to him, to last 32 days. Mr Beasley further announced that at the end of March they were to be given an additional 1d a day and, slowly, funds also started arriving from home. Some of them received 6s 8d as back pay too. Clothing could now be bought and they also set up coffee and tea stalls and made goods to sell like the French prisoners.

Alterations and repairs continued, but the volume of work was easing. The hole made in the wall to the outside privy by the would-be escapees needed repairs. It was decided to line the outside walls with elm planks and to put a strong door on the privy. Sentry boxes were to be fitted with wooden slides to the peep holes and gates were to be fitted at the south guard with a wicket.

By mid-February, the roofs of the Prisons needed reslating, partly for which prisoners were employed, and repairs were necessary for the back kitchen of one of the turnkey's houses at a cost of £2.

Shortly after, Capt Shortland was allowed to authorise a footway to the church which was under construction, and to the straw house, and to build a machine with a cart body on trucks for the carriage of the flat moor stone for paving the lower storeys of the Prisons, at a cost of £9. The footway was completed by early April when permission was given to extend it into Princetown.

A report in March revealed that four government-owned horses were constantly employed either in drawing stones for the Prison floors, church windows and churchyard walls or cleaning dung pits of the Prison yards. However, when the church and Prisons were completed, there was to be a reduction of one horse; three were considered absolutely necessary for other work.

Also in March, the shutters on the five older Prisons were repaired at a cost of £5 10s. Split fire grates were to be replaced with wrought iron ones in the Privates' guard room. In May prisoners were used to repair the prison boundary walls. In fact, Capt Shortland was given the order that 'the several works are to be proceeded with as expeditiously as possible while the Prisoners [French] remain'[91]

Shutters and stairs in the Prisons needed repairs by September, but the Board authorised only those occupied to be repaired, indicating that the Prisons were not full to capacity.

Also in September, all working parties were stopped due to the escape of prisoners Price and Vaughan.

Messrs Gill & Co supplied the blacksmiths shop with Welsh coals at 31s 6d per quarter.

Part of the iron railway that had been so necessary in the construction of the prison now seemed redundant. In April the Board told Capt Shortland to get the best possible bargain for it when negotiating the sale with the Bere Alston Mine Company who wanted to acquire it. Should this not be achieved, the railway was to be kept in store until further notice. It seems that the mine company was unsuccessful in its bid as the railway is referred to in later records.

Capt Shortland requested the use of a small enclosure of grassland of about an acre nearly opposite his residence in which to keep cows necessary for the use of his family.

Outside work for the prisoners was still permitted. In March, presumably on behalf of the

Turnpike Trust, Sir Thomas Tyrwhitt was allowed to employ forty prisoners 'in the formation of the Road between Dartmoor Prison and Plymouth'.[92] Two sentinels were to be employed - twenty prisoners to each. The mill adjoining Tor Royal, together with a piece of nearby land, was let to Mr Bennett in March, and he requested successfully that he could employ ten French bakers to assist him in his work.

Princetown, by now, had its first Post Office. The Board gave permission for John Arnold to be employed in the receiving and distributing of letters that passed through it.[93]

Ten days after 131 American prisoners arrived at Dartmoor in February, infection broke out again in Prison No.4. This time it was measles, confined to the American part of the building. It was decided that no more American prisoners should be received until the epidemic was over. A pneumonia outbreak also occurred in October, described as 'rife' by the Board, and many prisoners died. Capt Shortland's attempt to obtain shrouds for them was thwarted; 'We do not consider it necessary to inter the Bodies of the Prisoners in Shrouds, no Shrouds being provided for Seaman, belonging to H.M. Navy ships who may die'.[94]

There seems to have been a certain reluctance on the part of the prisoners to be admitted to the prison Hospital. According to Joseph Velpey (whose arrival is mentioned below), when first admitted, a prisoner was given a cold bath and then bled. It appears that they were compelled to give generously of their blood; 'I knew a Man that went into the hospital with a Bad cold and he at the first Bleeding had two hundred and forty ounces of Blood taken from him, the doctors here Makes a practice of Bleeding a person as long as he has Breath to draw'.[95]

Velpey's own reluctance to have medical treatment a few months into his confinement is apparent. 'On the twenty first [February 1815] I turned out inflicted with the tooth ache I went into the Receiving house with the Intent to have it taken out, but not liking the looks of the doctors mate I turned short round and came out and went into No. one prison and had three of my Jaw teeth taken out by a fellow prisoner'![96]

Religious instruction of the prisoners was not high on the list of the Board's priorities, although services were conducted informally amongst the prisoners. M. Le Villain, a French clergyman, requested the use of the surgeon's receiving house

The former Hospital. Note the blocked up original windows on the first floor.
© *Crown copyright NMR.*

when not occupied on public service for the purpose of holding services. But the Board denied this request. In November, they modified this decision, sending Capt Shortland a letter saying, 'A representation having been made to the Earl of Liverpool, that Divine Service has not been performed to the Prisoners in your Custody for 15 Months, we direct you to report if this Statement be correct, and whether The Revd Mr Mason has any objection to perform Divine Service to the Prisoners'.[97]

In February Capt Shortland had to report that the storehouse where the biscuits were kept was 'swarming with Rats', and in early May two hogsheads of beer to each Prison had been introduced. By December prisoners were allowed to buy strong beer - two hogsheads a week for each prison; however, there was to be no supply of spirits. But, in mid-December, Dr Baird reported to the Board that there was a great degree of drunkenness among the prisoners in Capt Shortland's care, and that he believed that the soldiers were smuggling in spirits! Indeed, Dr Magrath, speaking of his care of sick prisoners at Dartmoor said, 'They are exceedingly prone to dissipation, and undue-indulgence in spirituous potations';[98] a rather pompous way of saying that they were often drunk!

Supplies of alcoholic refreshment for civilians increased in 1814 too, with the Rundlestone Inn appearing for the first time in the records, under licensee Richard Hall, who may have been the supplier of moor stone as well.

It would seem that the profits from small beer had been stopped by January. Having had his income reduced as a direct result of this, John Mitchell, a Hospital clerk, applied to the Board for more coals for his sick mother and young sister for whom he had to provide.

Copper penny tokens had been introduced to the prisoners by farmers and tradesmen several years previously. However, prisoners were now complaining that they were no longer accepting them. This was dealt with promptly by the Board who denied access to the market of those farmers and tradesmen who had introduced them and now refused to take them back.

In August, the market was suspended due to the riotous behaviour of the prisoners.

Occupiers of the huts were again the source of annoyance to the Board. In mid April they asked Revd Mason the nature of the tenure of two of them by Messrs Carter (who must have had a reprieve or acquired another hut for himself) and Winn. It seems they were claiming 15 or 16 acres of prison land! Whatever his reply might have been, Capt Shortland was ordered to demolish them immediately, giving Carter and Winn only three days notice to remove their furniture. In August he was further ordered to cultivate the enclosure of land lately occupied by Carter for the benefit of the Government.

Napoleon had surrendered in April 1814 and had been sent to the island of Elba. Plans for the repatriation of French prisoners prompted the ordering of 6,000 leather shoes for them in late April. Capt Shortland also requested the hiring of wagons in addition to the Government one to take the ill ones to Plymouth. In mid-May, Capt Shortland was told 'your Depot should be cleared of Prisoners, with as little delay as possible'.[99] But he had to wait upon Capt Pellow, who had replaced Capt Rogers, at Mill Prison in Plymouth concerning the number of prisoners he could send at any one time.

Perez Drinkwater's letters mention the repatriation of the French prisoners:

'... yisterday [i.e. 19 May] they called up 500 French men to go away their was one that had been in prison Nine years and had worn his blanket out so that he had but half of it to give those rebels and on that acount they sent him back and put him on the bottom of the books for exchangeing, the man took it so hard that he cut his throught and was found dead between the prison dores, and a thousand other such deeds they have been guilty of since we have been confined heir in this cursed place and a monght these rebels for I can call them nothing better and I shall never dye happy till I have had the pleasure of killing one of them which I am determined to do if an oppertunity ever offers to me to doe it'.

With the removal of the French prisoners, numbers of Americans that could be housed increased. In June, the total number of American prisoners was 3,655, 'which number may be expected soon to increase'.[100] This was because the government decided to transfer other American prisoners of war to Dartmoor Prison. New hammocks were purchased at a cost of 5s 6d each and rugs at 2s 6d.

The black American prisoners, for some reason, became notorious for making life difficult for the others and, in 1814, all 90 of them were removed to the two upper floors of Prison No.4. According to Thomson, this was not on grounds of race but because theft by Negroes was rife. Richard Crafus, known as 'Big Dick' due to his height, was their leader. Joseph Velpey's journal (see below) records that 'Number four or the Middle Prison is for the Blacks in which there is Schools kept of all Descriptions such as Dancing Fencing Boxing and Music schools'.[101] Once all the French had been repatriated, badly behaved white men were sent to join the blacks.

This cockloft was the scene of a murder on the morning of 4 July, Independence Day. Prisoners Thomas Hill and James Henry had a prearranged fight in which Henry was killed. Hill, for some reason, was acquitted at Exeter Assize and returned to the Prison. In the meantime, the 4 July celebrations were allowed to continue.

Plans for an elaborate escape were started in August. Several American prisoners started to build tunnels under Prisons 4, 5 and 6. According to Daniel Alexander,

'they dug down about ten or twelve feet deep, and then ran what, in mining, is called an adit, under the bottoms of all the windings of this boundary-wall: they had measured their distance so accurately, that when they had got to the end of their adit, and were preparing to come to daylight, they just hit the inside of the boundary-wall instead of the outside: they were perceived by the sentry, on the ground gradually mouldering in, as sand does in an hour-glass'.[102]

The soil was disposed of in the water channels and under the limewash of the Prisons, Thomson claims this plan was betrayed by prisoner Bagley who traded the information for his freedom. The tunnellers were confined in Prisons 2 and 3 on two thirds rations. Years later, while digging the foundations for a prison building, one of the blocked up tunnels was discovered, filled with rubble put there shortly after discovery.

The despair felt by the Americans, fuelled by the weather and living conditions, is reflected in Perez Drinkwater's letter of 12 October:

'This same place is one of the most retched in this habbited world... neither wind nor water tight, it is situated on top of a high hill and is so high that it either rains, hails or snows almost the year round for further partickulars of my preasent unhappy situation, of my strong house, and my creeping friends [bedbugs and lice] which are without number.

I am compeled to smugle this out of prison for they will not allow us to write to our friends if they can help it... So I must conclude with telling you that I am not alone for their is almost 5,000 of us heir, and creepers a 1000 to one'.

Another American prisoner of war, Joseph Velpey, arrived in Plymouth on a prison ship on 29 October. He had been very ill and was relieved to be able to purchase bread, butter, milk and fruit which revived him somewhat. On 31 October, he and fellow prisoners were marched from Plymouth to Dartmoor Prison setting off at 7am and not arriving until 8.30pm. His journal describes a miserable journey in rain, on bad roads with many prisoners in a shoeless state, and the soldiers prodding them regularly with their bayonets. No food was provided and, upon their arrival, they were locked up, hungry and cold, in one of the Prisons.

In the morning, soldiers 'turned us Into the Yard for to Receive hammocks beds and Blankets that was as full of Lice as the Devil is of Wickedness'! Later that day, Velpey discovered about 500 men from his native Salem. He chose Prison No.7 in which to reside.

On 2 December American prisoner Nathaniel Pierce arrived and was, along with his fellow prisoners, put in Prison No.2 which had been empty. However, the following day, they were allowed to choose which Prison to stay in; meeting with someone he knew from back home, Nathaniel also chose No.7 which comprised 'a mess of my townsmen'.

His Journal gives interesting snippets of information such as two prisoners being tattooed on their cheeks 'for entering in to the British service from the Nasau prisson ship' (see the section on 1815), his vaccination against smallpox on 20 December, and a violent snow storm on the 26 December.

The removal of the French prisoners left a dearth of skilled labour. The Board rather liked Capt Shortland's suggestion that they employ the troops, saying 'should there be any Slaters among the Troops in Garrison at Dartmoor, we have no objection to their being employed to complete the Prison Roofs as you proposed'.[103] Whether the troops themselves approved is not recorded!

1815
Trouble brewing, a 'massacre within', arrivals and departures, new bulk supplies

Another fire, this time in the Hospital's drying house, broke out in mid-January. Although there was no serious damage, there was a loss of linen, and the repairs cost £29 14s 10d. Messrs Gill, Rundle & Co were paid £67 14s 6d for supplies of coal between 1 January and 30 June 1815.

The American prisoners continued to give the Board a run for their money. Towards the end of January they broke into the empty Prison No.6 and damaged the premises with a stolen iron bar. Capt Shortland demanded to know who was responsible but to no avail, so he threatened to stop the market. In turn, the prisoners refused to turn out of their Prisons for cleaning unless the market was reinstated, so their soup ration was stopped. This must have had the desired effect because, two days later, prisoners P.J. Cox, B. Hosgood, J. White and S. Squibb were all confined in the Cachot on short allowances to make good the damage.

In the meantime, prisoners Joseph Smith and John Price had letters forcibly tattooed on each cheek, US on one and T on the other, by some of the prisoners in Prison No.1. These letters stood for United States Traitor. They were sent to the Hospital while Capt Shortland attempted to find those responsible for the 'abominable transaction' to put in the Cachot. The Board, equally appalled, were anxious to prosecute them. By some means, Capt Shortland was partially successful

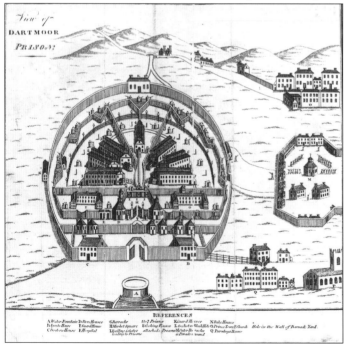

Dartmoor Prison in 1815 showing the Barracks, Church and the growing settlement of Princetown. *By permission of the British Library. Map c.38 e.37.*

as he found three culprits, J. Jackson, J. Hogaberts and S. Robinet, who were sent to trial in Exeter in March (although they are reputed to have been acquitted). From Joseph Velpey's journal it became apparent why at least one man was forcibly tattooed: On 17 January 'I went over to Number one prison for to see a fellow prisoner have two large Letters put into his Cheeks for being a Traitor to his Country and damning the flag'.[104] Thomson explains further by revealing they had served in the British Navy but had pleaded American citizenship to try and get an early release from duty.

Meting out their own punishments to fellow prisoners seemed standard practice with 'Juries' performing trials. Many of the sentences received were in the form of floggings. Velpey records several such incidents in his journal, for example; 'On the Ninth [December 1814] I went to see two Young Boys Floged for Stealing a Pound Note from there Mess Mates they Received two Dozen each on there Naked Backs Not for Stealing, but for being Cought'.[105] Also, on 13 January, another prisoner was sentenced to 48 lashes for stealing a great coat, but he fainted after 26 and was removed, with the intention of resuming after his recovery!

The prisoners, by now, were receiving regular religious instruction according to Nathaniel Pierce and Joseph Velpey. A preacher (from among the prisoners) preached to about forty mainly black prisoners every Sunday, while on Thursdays Mr Jones from Plymouth preached in the yard of Prison No.4. Interestingly, all gambling was halted on Good Friday (which fell on 23 March) in the 'Blacks Prison'.

Communications between prisoners in the Cachot and the Prison yard were brought to a halt in February with the erection of a paling from the Cachot wall to the inner wall of the Military Way. It was at this time that 200 extra men had been drafted in to the Garrison in consequence of the prisoners' riotous behaviour (see below).

Despite the winter, Dr Baird complained of the heat in the Prisons at 7.30am and said that when the temperature was 38° outside, the air in the lower floors had been about 56°, while the upper floors had been between 61° and 66°. He asked Capt Shortland whether ventilation was adequate in the Prisons. This coincided with an outbreak of smallpox and vaccines had to be obtained. On 2 February, 'the Doctors from the Hospital Made a Visit through all the prison's and desird all those that Never had the Small Pox for to be Noculated for to prevent this Infectious Disorder from Raging further'.[106] Smallpox also meant that prisoners were not permitted to have fires in their Prisons, thus tea kettles had to be boiled up in the Prison yards.

In May, prisoners were being admitted to the Hospital with 'rigid fingers' and on 6 May prisoner John Flowers died; at his Inquest, the jury returned a verdict of 'Died by the visitation of God'.

On 4 April 1,200 letters arrived mostly from the Marblehead and Salem areas of America on the sloop *Fortunate*, but none were for Joseph Velpey. His keen disappointment is felt when he wrote 'I hope that it May please the almighty God for to spare me that I may once more see My parents and know the reason for there Slighting me so much as they have done since I left Salem'.[107] Unhappily, Velpey died on his journey home so he never knew the reason; his journal survived for his parents to see this poignant entry, and one can only wonder what they must have felt upon reading it.

On 6 April 1815 a serious and subsequently famous incident occurred in which five American prisoners were shot dead (with another two dying within two days) and 34 were injured by the military (see Appendix III for a contemporary account). Capt Shortland's initial report said that he had not been able to ascertain the cause other than a dissatisfaction at being detained in England.

Events leading up to the massacre had resulted in an undercurrent of unrest. In 1814 four prisoners accused of trying to blow up a British schooner were landed and sent to the Cachot at Dartmoor Prison where the Admiralty said they were to stay for the remainder of the war. There was great sympathy for them from their fellow prisoners who smuggled a note to them saying they would be well hidden if they managed to break into the Prison. On 13 February 1815 one of the prisoners, Simeon Hayes, achieved this and was initially smuggled into No.1 Prison and then into No.4 where he was blackened with soot to look like a Negro.

The escapee eluded the militia, and the prisoners were threatened with the closure of the market which is what happened. Eventually Hayes was betrayed, but a search of No.5, where he was now hidden, was fruitless. The prisoners, in riotous mood, were turned out and threatened with no water until he was given up. They refused to return to the prison, saying that as water could be obtained in the yard, they would stay there.

A stone thrown at Capt Shortland's cheek provoked him to give the order to fire. The Captain of the militia gave a counter-command and Capt Shortland left the yard, probably realising he had made an unwise move.

Hayes remained at large for a few more days until he was recognised by the Cachot keeper, James Carley, and re-incarcerated in it. Ten days later Hayes and his three co-prisoners were removed from Dartmoor. But the simmering unrest stayed, fuelled by bad food and conditions.

Perez Drinkwater wrote a letter to his parents on 8 April, shortly before his departure from Dartmoor Prison, in which he touches upon the events of 6 April.

'It was one of the most retched things that ever took place Amonghts the savages much more amonghts peple that are the bullwarks of our religion. I had the good fortin to escape their fury, but they killed some while begging for mercy after being wounded they likewise kicked and mangle the dead right before our faces. Pain Perry of North Yarmouth was one that was wounded but not bad... one of our Crew was killed in the Late Marseehree [massacre] his name was James Man'.

Prisoner accounts of the numbers of prisoners in the vicinity of the massacre vary considerably: Perez Drinkwater claims it was 5,000, while Pierce says it was 300.

An insight into the numbers and the employment of prisoners at this time was given by Andrews. He recorded that on 10 April:

Prison No.1 - 1,290	Employed in stores and Hospital - 29
No.3 - 952	Patients in Hospital - 107
No.4 - 978	Coloured prisoners - 1,000
No. 5 - 938	
No.7 - 1,248	

Labourer Robert Evely was sacked in May for neglect of duties.

By late May/early June the American prisoners were starting to be repatriated in large numbers, with 366 discharged from Dartmoor. In expectation of his departure, on 5 May, Nathaniel Pierce sold his hammock to buy shoes for his march to Plymouth - otherwise he would have had to have gone barefoot! In the event, he did not leave Dartmoor until early July. He was thus able to record a bull baiting on the morning of 23 May, in sight of the prison.

Capt Shortland was informed that 'Lieut Cheeseman [of Stonehouse] has been ordered to embark the whole of the American Prisoners with as little Delay as possible on the Arrival of vessels which are on their way to Plymouth for their Reception'.[108] Capt Shortland was to send as many prisoners as Lieut Cheeseman wanted, but to detain the sick prisoners until last. By 4 June another 273 prisoners had been discharged and, by 29 June this number had risen to a further 1,082.

> We'll bid adieu to Dartmoor there Potatoes Coal and Turf
> There barley Bread and Turnips and dam'n Doctors stuff
> There codfish and herrin no more of that we'll use
> But leave it behind for Doctors clerks Turnkey's and Jews
>
> Fare well you sharks of dartmoor the day at length arrives
> Behold the Yankey's marching with tears all in your eyes
> Adieu my loving Countrymen that behind the walls do lay
> But your scotch and Irish Doctors no more of us shall slay
>
> *Joseph Velpey*

Despite these departures for their homeland, escapes continued apace. 30 had escaped from the Prison but had reappeared in Plymouth ready for repatriation! Lamplighter Charles Shipley had been confined due to helping American prisoner W. Webster escape from the Prison.

With so many departures, repairs to the Prisons 1, 2 and 3 were put on hold. But towards the end of June Capt Shortland received the communication from the Board that he was to prepare for the immediate reception of 5,000 French prisoners, who were to be kept separate from the remaining Americans. Napoleon's escape from Elba in March had meant that war had resumed between France and Britain with many prisoners being taken again.

The decision not to do the repairs was hurriedly reversed, and Prisons 4,5,6 and 7 were also whitewashed, and the Hospital doors were painted. With repairs and building work continuing, by September, Capt Shortland had to ask permission for Herne Hole Quarry to continue being worked, which was granted.

Bedding for 5,000 prisoners was also washed and cleaned with more ordered for a possible total of 8-9,000, and the Prisons and Hospital were fumigated. All unserviceable articles from the prison were to be sent to Lieut Cheeseman 'after they shall have been cleaned at Horrabridge, in order that they might be sent round to Deptford'[109] while old linen items were to go to Capt Hutchinson at Mill Prison.

With the arrival of 209 French prisoners on 1 July came one French woman, closely followed by three others in the next intakes, which posed something of a problem but the order was given that they should be victualled for the time being.

Sick prisoners arriving at Plymouth were looked after at Mill Prison until they were fit. Capt Shortland was advised to send the Prison's wagon to Plymouth once a week to collect those prisoners who were recovered but not able to walk.

Throughout July American prisoners continued to be released while French prisoners continued to be received; the last American prisoner was released on 24 July. By the end of the month, Capt Shortland had to report to the Board that the prison buildings were swarming with rats and that he was having to employ another ratcatcher from the Dock Yard at Plymouth.

The huge influx of prisoners meant the numbers of militia had to be maintained and even increased. A report shortly after the prison had closed, highlights the growing problem of supplying troops for the Garrison. Col. Wood of the East Middlesex Militia said that his troops received the order to march to Dartmoor, 'which they did; and there being a scarcity of troops on that part of the country at the time, they were not permitted to rendezvous at Plymouth, where it had been the custom to assemble regiments in general previous to taking the duty of Dartmoor, but they went immediately from their march to that station'.[110]

Victualling all these prisoners resulted in new contracts; for example, Johnathan Birch obtained one for victualling sick prisoners: 'the Prices at which the said Contract is taken are for Low Diet sixpence, Half Diet One Shilling & eight Pence; & Full Diet One Shilling & ten Pence'.[111]

Problems with the victuallers did not go away. Supplies of cod fish were claimed to be hard to procure and beef had to be substituted for three weeks in September. However, the situation had not improved by October, and the contractor, Mr Sharman, was told that the Newfoundland Fishery had not been affected by an Act of Parliament and, unless he supplied cod and herrings regularly, he would be severely dealt with.

The store clerk, John Bennett, requested a pay rise in August. The Board said that if he 'will give security by Two respectable Sureties joining him in a Bond for £200, we will approve him Storekeeper of the Depot, with a Salary of £30 per Annum in addition to his present pay, and he will then be certainly charged with all the Stores'.[112] This seemed to meet with Mr Bennett's

approval as he put forward the Revd R.K. Willesford and F. Willesford Esq, both of Tavistock, as his sureties.

One of the surviving stores/military prisons, now housing the Governor's office.
Elisabeth Stanbrook.

In September Capt Shortland asked for 2-3,000 suits of clothing and he was given permission to order enough to ensure there were 4,000 in store. He also ordered clog shoes and, just over a month later in November, another 4,000 pairs of shoes plus 4,000 blankets.

Illness was still a problem. Dr Baird had visited the prison again and ordered some forms for the sick prisoners to sit on, together with 120 cradles, and also asked for another hospital mate to be appointed; this was Mr R. Dick who took up the post on 24 September. In October smallpox, measles and 'scarletina' were present, and Dr Magrath, who had replaced Mr Dyker in September 1814, asked for vaccines from the Royal Hospital at Plymouth as some of the children of the East Middlesex Militia had smallpox.

The new intake of French prisoners were still just as keen to sell or gamble away their clothing and, by late November, Capt Shortland was ordered to re-clothe the culprits and put them on a short allowance to pay for them. A month later he reported that most of those in the Hospital were those with no clothes left, and that the unoccupied wards of the Hospital could be used to house them, with only small fires allowed to prevent further misdemeanour! Gambling and selling clothing was acceptable among the prisoners, but theft was not. One prisoner, J. Pierre, had been flogged by fellow prisoners for stealing 4 pairs of 'pantaloons'; another had been flogged for an unspecified crime at the same time and was in hospital. The Board directed them to take any complaints to Capt Shortland, and that they were to be publicly apprised.

The severity of the cold and damp in the Cachot during December was causing some concern to Dr Magrath, who said that being confined within it would endanger lives and necessitate hospital treatment. The Board said if this was so, no one was to be put in it.

By December 1815, after Napoleon's defeat at Waterloo, the end of the complex as a War Prison was in sight. In a letter to Revd Mason the Board said they wished to 'acquaint you that as the whole of the Establishment will soon be abolished, the Board do not feel themselves authorised to incur any further Expense at present'.[113] Capt Shortland was informed that vessels to take the French prisoners away would come up the Hamoaze and that the prisoners were to be embarked at Lopwell Quay instead of Plymouth if he approved. But he didn't, and they went to Plymouth instead.

1816
The end in sight

January 1816 saw the departure of many French prisoners. The vast amounts of redundant bedding were, if particularly foul, to be cleaned at Horrabridge, otherwise they were to go straight to Plymouth.

There was now a need for fewer men in the Garrison - fifty 'Rank and File' were considered sufficient to take care of the buildings. The Board informed Capt Shortland on 2 February that the establishment must be entirely 'abolished' by 20 February and that the premises would then be 'delivered into the charge of Mr Walters, and all the Stores to be left in the charge of Mr Bennett by Inventory'.[114] The only remaining personnel were to be eight Hospital patients who could not be removed, and one volunteer nurse to attend them (all prisoners). Some turnkeys and labourers were also to remain until further notice.

Capt Shortland was to move to temporary accommodation at Lipson Cottage near Plymouth, and he obtained permission to use the government-owned wagons to transport his furniture there when he left after 20 February. He then moved to Surrey Street, The Strand before returning to Plymouth.

The eight sick prisoners and their nurse were taken to Plymouth on 6 February, accompanied by Mr P. Coleman who received travelling expenses of £1 14s. Mr Dick, who accompanied these prisoners to France was paid £10 6s expenses. The dispenser's store was consequently packed up and left there in charge of the storekeeper.

Mr Carpenter, who currently rented the slaughterhouse, asked that his rent might cease on account of the prisoners' departure, and the Board agreed to this. However, Captain Humphries requested that the butcher who supplied the troops might be allowed the use of the premises. This was agreed to but its use was short-lived due to the removal of most of the troops in March.

The Board offered Messrs Gill & Co of Tavistock further occupation of the bakehouse in Tavistock Road in March, but they declined the offer. After all, with another bakehouse on Two Bridges Road, who would now buy their large quantities of bread?

Wagons and horses were sent to Plymouth to be sold by Lieut Cheeseman, and on 14 February the turnkeys and labourers were given one week's notice to quit their houses.

The 20 February arrived at last. Capt Shortland wrote to the Board saying that he had paid off all of the establishment, leaving Mr Walters in charge of the premises and Mr Bennett of the stores. The latter hired wagons and carts to take some of the stores to Stonehouse. This process took about nine days, aided by former staff: Messrs D. Pilmore, W. Norris, W. May, J. Halfyard, R. Arnold, D. Nichols, J. Rodd, G. Challacombe and T. Physick, who were each paid a labourer's wage for this work.

Throughout 1816 stores continued to be removed to Plymouth for dispersal either by the Transport Office or the Barrack Board. In June Mr Bennett found himself in a spot of bother, a past misdemeanour having caught up with him. Three months earlier the Board had given him £130 to pay the bills of people removing the stores, but he had only paid them by bankers drafts which had not been honoured. Mr Adams of the Board was sent down to Dartmoor from London to take charge of the stores and Mr Bennett was informed that his services were no longer required.

The iron railway had never been sold and this, together with other iron, steel and lead were to be left in charge of the Barrack Master, and an auction organised for its sale by a reputable auctioneer.

Having to vacate his house, Mr Holmden asked that he might take with him the range and oven, and shrubs from the garden.

The prison was not in good repair and in mid-March, Mr Walters suggested that two masons and two carpenters be allowed to repair it. The Board agreed to this but stipulated that necessary repairs only were to be made. An allowance could also be made for lighting the lamps. Further permission was granted in April to repair the gable ends of the old Prisons.

Mr Walters' pay for July was £9 6s and £9 10s for August, to include 4s for two days pay to the labourers. After receiving his September pay of £9, he was told that his pay would cease at the end of the present quarter.

At the end of August, a list of stores still at large included 4,090 bricks, 2,850 laths, over a ton of lead and 4 'Stourbridge Lumps'.

In March the Board asked Mr Bennett and Mr Walters to enquire about the population in the vicinity of the prison, within a three mile radius of the church, exclusive of the remaining troops. Their answer is revealing about the local population that had grown up around the prison: 92 men, 119 women, 64 boys and 105 girls.

1817
Final costs, final plans

There were only about two entries of any significance in the Admiralty records for 1817. The first, dated 8 January, reveals that Mr Walters' last pay in December 1816 had been £9 6s, and he was also told to draw upon the Transport Office for £109 4s 'being the Amount of the Gratuity allowed to you as stated in our letter to you of 26th October last'.[115]

The second entry is on 30 October when it showed that the whole of the department had been transferred to the Victualling Board.

And so ended the first phase of Dartmoor Prison's history; the scene of so much suffering by human beings whose only 'crime' had been to defend their country and be caught by the enemy. According to Thomson, who quoted from the records, a total of 1,478 prisoners died during their incarceration here, 280 of them Americans, although the figure is now thought to be slightly higher. Their bones are buried in two separate cemeteries; one each dedicated to the Americans and the French. The original burying ground proved inadequate in the longterm. In the mid-1860s, pigs that had been reared within the convict prison boundary were turned out on the former burial field (and future gasworks field) began to routle up bones and coffins of dead prisoners, and they lay on the surface becoming sun bleached and weathered. The decision was taken to create two cemeteries, and all the bones were excavated and divided, somewhat arbitrarily, into two groups and re-interred accordingly. Obelisks were then erected at each cemetery, and today the sites are maintained. They remain tributes to the men who suffered as only Dartmoor can make men suffer, and they will not be forgotten.

The final cost of building the prison was 'About £127,000; that sum having saved to the public... £56,000, being the difference between using the stone quarries on the spot, and building with brick or any other material'.[116]

Interestingly, the first plan to use Dartmoor Prison for convicts was mooted in 1815. On 18 February the Transport Board wrote to Lord Viscount Sidmouth suggesting that as soon as the

The French prisoner of war cemetery.
Elisabeth Stanbrook.

The American prisoner of war cemetery.
Elisabeth Stanbrook.

The small cross on the wall of Prison No.1, dedicated to a prisoner who was shot dead nearby. *Elisabeth Stanbrook.*

Prison No.1, converted into a cell block in the late 19th century.
© *Crown copyright NMR.*

Part of the original market wall and pillar.
Elisabeth Stanbrook.

Americans had been released, could not the prison be used for housing convicts destined for transportation to New South Wales? Prisoners shipped out in winter months were susceptible to dying due to the cold and extremes of temperatures as they sailed through changes of climates. Indeed, one ship called the *Surrey* had arrived in New South Wales, Australia with the loss of fifty prisoners. To hold them at Dartmoor until the spring would be better, and Plymouth was very convenient for sailings. This plan never came to fruition.

Of the original prison buildings little remain. Prison No.1 (now F Block) has been much altered and extended and, high up on the original exterior wall is a small cross put there by prisoners in memory of another who was shot dead outside a nearby door. Prison No.4 survives, with its clerestory, having been used as a chapel and a cinema/theatre; Prison No.6 was much reduced in height in the 1940s and used as a kitchen for a while. The Petty Officers' Prison (turned into a chapel and a hospital) and the Hospital (turned into workshops) also survive although, again, much altered; and the two polygonal stores/military prisons are still there. Original moor stone flooring can also be seen in some of these buildings.

Part of a wall that surrounded the market square remains as do the Agent's and surgeon's houses which have undergone extensive alterations. Other buildings were demolished and rebuilt, and E Wing was built on the site of the bathing pool. The inner and outer gateways, the circular perimeter wall and the reservoir are now listed buildings, as are other internal prison buildings. The Barracks were nearly all demolished with just blocks 1, 10 (Grosvenor House) and 11 (Dart Cottage) remaining, although heavily altered.

The former Barracks No.1.
Elisabeth Stanbrook.

Grosvenor House which was once Barracks No.10.
Elisabeth Stanbrook.

Dart Cottage, formerly Barracks No.11.
Elisabeth Stanbrook.

Detail of the gatepost and surviving lower hinge on
Dart Cottage (Barracks No.11).
Elisabeth Stanbrook.

Princetown Church

Several accounts have been written about the church but they have been based upon secondary sources, and hence inaccuracies have become 'facts'. For example, it is generally accepted that the church was designed by Daniel Asher Alexander, the architect responsible for the prison; that building commenced in 1810; and that the American prisoners were responsible only for the interior of the church. The early history of Princetown Church is usually referred to only briefly, most published accounts concentrating on the church after the prison became used for housing civilian convicts from 1850 onwards. This chapter attempts to redress the balance, examining the actual erection of the church, together with the adjoining Parsonage House, and dispelling the long-standing misconceptions.

In 1791 there was an unsuccessful attempt to pass a Bill to divide the Forest of Dartmoor into two, thus forming a new parish.[117] This parish, to have been called St George, was to have a new church built at Two Bridges. This Bill was defeated but the desire for the church remained and in 1797 John Swete saw plans of it in the possession of Judge Buller, at Prince Hall.[118] Interestingly, the site for this church appears on the Ordnance Surveyors' Drawings for 1802-3.[119] It was to be built near to where Roundhill Cottage stands, on the Two Bridges to Princetown road. In the meantime, services for the locality were being held at Prince Hall and, later, in an unconsecrated barn at Beardown Farm,[120] no doubt conducted by Revd Bray, Mr Bray's son.

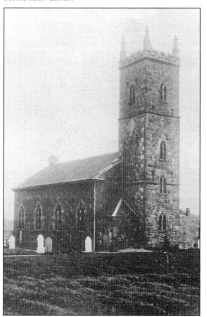

An early photograph of Princetown Church before renovations.

The church at Two Bridges did not get built. Judge Buller died in 1800 and by 1805 Tyrwhitt had made extensive plans to build the War Prison on his land at Princetown, and this included a chapel.[121] This chapel, which in fact was always referred to as 'Dartmoor Church' in the records, was to be for the use of the militia and their families, and the local population.

Plans to build this church at Dartmoor had still not come to fruition by November 1811, and Capt Isaac Cotgrave was compelled to confirm the Board's suspicion that the erection of one had not even been started. In response to this, the Board instructed Capt Cotgrave to make enquiries as to the number of people it would be proper for such a church to accommodate; the answer was 500-600.[122]

On 10 January 1812 Capt Cotgrave received notification that the Lord Commissioners of the Admiralty had authorised the Board to erect a church and a house for the clergyman who was to be appointed to perform divine service. It is from these records that we learn that the architect was not Mr Alexander but Mr John Walters, Foreman of the Works at Dartmoor. He was instructed 'to draw a Plan and Elevation of the said Church and House which are to be executed upon the plainest, and most economical style possible. The Church to contain about 5 or 600 people, and the House to be sufficient for a Clergyman and his wife having a Parlor [sic] - Dining Room - 4 Bedrooms - Kitchen etc. The whole to be built of the moor or granite stone by Assistance of the necessary Number of French Prisoners so that the whole may be executed in the course of the summer.'[123] The hope that even one of these might be completed by the summer was rather optimistic on the part of the Board, as they were to discover.

Initially, it was thought the best place to site the Parsonage House would be to the north of the church, thus shielding it from the inclement south west weather. But this idea was shelved when the Admiralty let Capt Cotgrave and John Walters site it where they wished. This was to the south-west, as contemporary plans show. The land to the north was in possession of two labourers, probably Whiteway and Norman, who were reluctant to relinquish it; the more modern Chaplain's House, built c.1860-1[124] stands there today.

Inside the church, 'common forms [i.e. benches] with Backs should be constructed for general use, and some inclosed Seats for the Principal Officers and their Families'.[125] The churchyard was to be 1¹/₂ acres, with the enclosing of a parade for the troops to assemble or separate. The back part of the house 'may be possibly constructed with an High Roof as better calculated to resist the prevailing Weather'.[126]

The initial estimate submitted by Mr Walters was, despite the Board's call for economy, thought to be rather cheap. They therefore ordered him to prepare another plan and elevation incorporating a gallery. No tower was deemed necessary at this point, 'merely a Belfrey [sic] for 1 Bell'.[127] However, by November 1812, the Board had changed their minds and recommended that there should be a tower 'perpendicular to its height instead of the Capola [sic] Form, on account of its exposed situation and that Three Cast Iron Frames with grooves to take pane[s] of Glass should be fixed in each Window'.[128] The stone necessary for the building was to be drawn by government horses, and records suggest that much of the granite may have come from Herne Hole Quarry.

On 12 February 1812 Capt Cotgrave was instructed to proceed with the building of the church but on 22 February this order was retracted while further consideration was given to Mr Walters' estimate. Eventually, on 19 March 1812 Capt Cotgrave received the orders for work on the church to start, several years after it had first been planned.

In November 1812 decisions about the roof materials had to be made. According to Mr Walters' estimates, a lead roof would cost £612 and a slate roof £135. It need hardly be said that the Board chose the latter. Louis Leroy was appointed to help Mr Walters with the roofing.

Since 1807 Revd James Holman Mason, not a man to miss a business opportunity, had been conducting divine service on Sundays for the workmen employed in building the prison. He had taken it upon himself to inclose one of the airing sheds and appropriate it for Sunday worship,

Revd James Holman Mason, a business opportunist as well as a vicar.
Courtesy Stephen Woods.

with 200 people attending the services.[129] In May 1809, upon the impending arrival of the prisoners, he had applied to the Board to use part of the prison Hospital for his services. This was denied him by return, the Board expressing some surprise that he had been taking services on prison property at all. They informed him that their department made available no such facility for prisoners of war and that the Regiment of Militia on duty at the prison would probably have their own chaplain.

Not to be deterred, Revd Mason continued with his services for the workmen, as can be seen from the Baptismal Register. He was thus in a good position to apply for the post of Minister at Dartmoor Church which, in due course, he did. On 13 April 1813 the Board confirmed his appointment to this post, and on 28 April they sent him a letter giving details of his salary which was to be £300 per annum payable from the time the church would be open for divine service. This was later altered to commence from the date of his appointment.

Despite Revd Mason's appointment, it was to be several months before the church was opened for divine service. Problems with supplies of materials were the main cause of delay. By August 1813 neither church nor Parsonage House were anywhere near completion, much to the Board's consternation. The supplier of lead, Mr Bryant, had not produced the badly needed goods. Mr Walters was waiting for 12 rolls of common sheet lead - 7lb to a foot - and 2 rolls of common sheet lead -14lb to a foot. Mr Bryant's excuses were not sympathetically received by the Board. He was told that either he supplied the lead immediately or they would purchase it elsewhere at his cost. Towards the end of October, the lead was still conspicuous by its absence. Capt Cotgrave therefore had to buy 6 rolls from Mr Husband of Plymouth Dock to tide them over.

About this time, Revd Mason was negotiating for a 7 feet stone wall to be built around the churchyard. The Board agreed to the wall but reduced the size to 5 feet. In the meantime, Mr Walters was equally keen to negotiate the building of a shed near the church walls to shelter the stone cutters from the frequently inclement weather. This was also granted.

The church and Parsonage House were still not finished in January 1814. Despite this, Revd Mason performed divine service for the first time in the church on 2 January of that year. Burt, writing only a few years later in 1826[130] erroneously claims this to have been in 1815, but the Baptismal Register clearly shows otherwise. After this first service, Revd Mason baptised two children, Caroline Mason Broderick, daughter of a Plymouth merchant, and Thomas Luckey Jewell, son of a husbandman living at Princetown brewery.

As the interior of the church had not even been begun, conditions inside must have been extremely makeshift and uncomfortable! Mr Walters was appointed Clerk of the Church at a salary of £20 per annum while John Kirton was appointed Sexton at £10 per annum.[131]

The building of the church and Parsonage House continued. Cast iron frames, necessary to complete the church roof, were ordered from 'Mount Foundry' in Tavistock. Window frames were to be ordered, fitted in and glazed. April 1814 did at least see the completion of the footpath between the prison and the church and permission was granted to extend this into Princetown.

Up until May 1814, labour for the building work came from among the French prisoners who were paid 6d per day. However, upon their departure in mid-May, American prisoners, who had arrived at the prison in 1813, were permitted to take their places in the working parties. Capt Shortland, who had replaced Capt Cotgrave in November 1813, was instructed to use those who were 'Carpenters, Masons and Blacksmiths to proceed with the Works at the Church and Parsonage House, and you are to report at the end of one Month, the Conduct of the Prisoners who you may so employ'.[132] It is these original records which correct published histories by showing that Americans were responsible for the building of some of the church exterior too, including the tower and the church walls. Americans also worked on the Parsonage House and Glebe walls. In fact, it was not until September 1814 that plans for the interior of the church were even considered by the Board. As well as the official Board records, a contemporary account by the American prisoner, Charles Andrews, confirms that his fellow countrymen were put to work on the church. Andrews recorded that Capt Shortland

'told the prisoners that he had orders to employ any number of the prisoners he should think necessary; such as carpenters and masons to build a church near the prison ... if any prisoner attempted to make his escape, [that] no more Americans would be employed ... they were to receive six-pence per day, every three months, and if any prisoner escaped, the whole pay was forfeited'.[133]

An elaborate escape plan concerning the Parsonage House is related by Capt Vernon Harris, one time Governor of the Dartmoor Convict Prison. A prisoner was employed as a mason working on a flue intended for an open fireplace. Once it had reached a certain height, a cavity was formed just large enough to accommodate a man. The outer face was then filled in with thin stone. Once built up above the cavity, the flue was rendered in mortar with spaces left for air and observation. On the intended day of escape, the prisoner concealed himself in the cavity and fellow prisoners then 'finished' the flue. 'They took so much pains to ensure a creditable appearance as to draw forth the commendations of the instructor, who complimented them upon this improved face put on the work'.[134]

The prisoner was missed at roll-call, and a thorough search of the Parsonage House which included bayonets being thrust into the flue, revealed nothing. Concluding that the prisoner had escaped, he was able to break out of the thin walls that night and disappear into the dark.

In July, Revd Mason received a letter from the Board allowing him to order two bibles and two prayer books for the church. The cost was not to exceed £10 13s. Interior fitments were also needed. A pulpit and desk in St Sidwell's Church, Exeter, for sale at £22, were purchased.[135] The oak pulpit is eighteenth century with carvings of the four evangelists on it. Also, two Portland

The 18th century pulpit from St Sidwell's Church, Exeter.
Elisabeth Stanbrook.

The church font crafted by Mr Winnie.
Elisabeth Stanbrook.

stone chimney pieces, for two rooms in the church, were bought at a cost of £2 each, and 10s for the fitting. A plan for a specially made font was sent to the Board by Revd Mason. They agreed to pay the craftsman, Mr Winnie, £15 for it but they would not provide the tools. Two surplices, costing £7 18s 3d, were also ordered.

In September 1814 a wall around the churchyard was to be built before consecration of the church. However, due to the escape of prisoners Price and Vaughan, all working parties had been stopped, in accordance with the conditions. Instead, the militia were called upon to complete this wall!

A coach from London arrived at the prison on 3 October delivering a box for Revd Mason, containing the following: a folio Church Bible in two volumes, two folio Prayer Books for Church Service, a Book for Communion Service and a Book of Church Offices, Baptisms, Burials, etc. It would appear that the Board had no idea that Revd Mason had already conducted divine service at Dartmoor Church because, on 21 December 1814, they wrote to him asking when the church would be ready for this purpose. His answer is not recorded.

Meanwhile, supplies were still being ordered, including velvet cushions and hassocks. This constant demand was stretching the patience of the Board. At the end of December they wrote to

Interior of the church before
alterations.

Capt Shortland saying, 'We cannot but express our surprise that such frequent Application should be made to us on Account of the Articles wanted for the Use of the Church, which might with more propriety have been included in one general Demand'.[136] Revd Mason was undeterred by this and on 10 January 1815 he asked the Board for one or two sweeping brushes, two hand scrubbing brushes, one with a handle, a few coarse cloths, a mop or two, one or two water pails, some soap, a set of plain fire irons, and a hearth brush for the two rooms, a table, a few chairs and a looking glass for the clergyman's room and a church clock. The Board refused the soap and the fire irons. They allowed the rest, and he was to get a small deal table and three rush-bottomed chairs. In addition, there was to be an allowance of 1½ bushels of coal per week for each of the 'Brodies' stoves in the winter, and 1 bushel in the summer to keep the church aired. The clerk's reading desk and pulpit had arrived by March 1815 and Capt Shortland was directed by the Board to pay the packaging charge of £2 14s. It would appear from the records that the church was at long last finished.

The situation was rather different with the Parsonage House and church walls. It was not until May 1815 that the house was ready to be plastered, and a plasterer was duly employed at the rate of 3s per day. In September Revd Mason asked for a stable and cow house to be erected in the grounds of the house, the work to be carried out by the prisoners. The estimate was £111 16s, a sum too great for the Board to consider, so this plan was dropped. This correspondence referred to the Parsonage House as still 'being built'. By mid-October the end was in sight; all that was needed to complete the House were chimney pieces, slabs and grates.

The burying ground was consecrated on 1 November 1815.[137] Mr Thomas Turner, Chaplain to the Bishop of Exeter, sent Revd Mason the bill for this service amounting to £19 15s 6d, and was instructed by the Board to pay it by the end of November. Revd Mason was still sending the Board orders for items for the church. Early in December he asked them for a communion plate. Their answer reflects the running down of the prison due to the end of hostilities and the repatriation of prisoners: 'I am directed by the Board to acknowledge the receipt of your letter of 10th Instant, relative to the purchase of Communion Plate for the use of the Church at Dartmoor, and in return to acquaint you that as the whole of the Establishment will soon be abolished, the Board do not feel themselves authorised to incur any further Expense at present'·[138] The church bells, although cast, were not installed in the tower - another expense spared, no doubt. Instead they were taken from Plymouth to the Dockyard and hung in a chapel there.

References to the church in the Admiralty Board's records cease in 1816, except those made to authorise Mr Alexander Adams of the Board to permit Revd Mason to have the coals in the stores for the use of the church. Other references were for the drawing of his quarterly pay in July and October.

So it would seem that the church, and indeed the Parsonage House, were finished in time for the closure of the War Prison and the departure of all troops and associated staff. As the church was built largely for the use of the prison personnel, the Board may well have regretted the whole exercise, especially had they foreseen that their initial plan for it to be finished in the summer of 1812 had been an impossible dream. They may have considered it fortunate that some services did take place in the church, albeit surrounded by building materials and devoid of many internal fittings and fixtures.

Although there was a mass exodus of civil and military personnel from Princetown, local people remained in some of the dwellings, and the Barracks which had housed the troops, and the Parsonage House, were, in time, leased to the nearby quarry owners at Foggintor to accommodate their workers.

The memorial window dedicated to the Americans who were confined in Dartmoor Prison during the War of 1812.
Elisabeth Stanbrook.

The history of the church continues, of course, and it became used as a chapel of ease for the Dartmoor Quarter of Lydford parish. Throughout the ensuing years, it has been much altered and enlarged, both inside and out.

In June 1908, a New York newspaper reported that a church in England, partly built by the American prisoners of war, was falling into a state of disrepair and funds were badly needed to restore it. This report caught the attention of the president, Mrs Slade, of the National Society of United States Daughters of 1812, whose remit is to commemorate those who died in the War of 1812. The 3,000 strong membership donated £250 for the memorial window in the east wall of the church. It depicts the birth, life, death and resurrection of

Christ in seven panels. The inscription at the bottom reads:

'To the glory of God and in memory of the American prisoners of war who were detained in the Dartmoor war prison between the years 1813-15, and who helped to build the church, especially of the 218 brave men who died here on behalf of their country, this window is presented by the National Society of United States Daughters of 1812. Dulce est pro patria mori'.

Two years later, in June 1910, a special ceremonial service took place at which the window was unveiled. Mrs Slade, representing the Society, came over from America to perform the deed. She also presented to the rector, Revd Heathcote Smith, a special certificate containing a copy of the window's inscription.

The ongoing history of Princetown Church has been recorded elsewhere but recent events are worthy of mention here. In 1994, it acquired notoriety through its redundancy and closure. Necessary repairs were considered too costly by the bodies responsible for its upkeep, and the Grade II* church stood forlornly within its churchyard awaiting a decision on its future. It was on the market facing demolition if not sold, which would have been a tragedy as it is of international significance, its links with France and America being of particular importance.

Happily, the church was taken over by The Churches Conservation Trust in 2000, and the building has been saved. Three initial phases of work, sponsored by the Department for Culture, Media and Sport and the Church of England, were then planned to put the church into good repair. Phase I included repair and consolidation of the tower walls, replacement of the tower roof and floor, the introduction of a staircase for access to the windows, floors and roof by maintenance and Trust staff, and repairs to windows. Phase II concentrated on external elevations, drainage and roof of the rest of the church, while Phase III involves repairs to the interior fixtures and fittings.

Appendix I
The Foul Leat and Water Courses

S upplying water to the prison was via a leat taken off the River Walkham, which was further supplemented by the Spriddle Lake, about 4 miles north of the prison. The head weir is an interesting feature with elaborate stone work and the straightening of a small stretch of the river. This leat culminated in a reservoir to the west of the prison buildings and then was channelled through the prison complex, as described in the section on 1812. The carrying away of 'foul water' was not such an easy matter. Both seemed fraught with problems.

Early in 1808 Mr Tyrwhitt, who was cultivating land on his Tor Royal estate, became interested in the 'foul water' from the prison as he saw it as a means of fertilising his lands by the construction of a 'foul leat'. Prior to his interest this foul water was destined for the Blackabrook, being channelled either over or under the Devonport Leat which was owned by the Plymouth Dock Water Company (PDWC).

The Board's response to Tyrwhitt's enquiry was that they 'were willing to convey at Expense of Government the Water from the Prison at Dartmoor direct to the Blackabrook either over or under the Company's Leat as the Comp^y might think proper but if neither would be allowed the Water must of Necessity be conveyed to the Grounds of Mr Tyrwhitt in the Manner requested by him'.[139] They seemed rather reluctant to accommodate Tyrwhitt's plan but did agree to set up a meeting on 30 May between representatives of the Board, Messrs Bowen and Douglas, Mr Alexander (who was working for the Elder Brethren at Trinity House) and the PDWC.

This meeting did not go according to Tyrwhitt's plan. On the recommendation of Bowen and Douglas, the Board decided to adopt whichever plan the PDWC favoured. By mid-June, the Board were informed that 'the Dock Company preferred the Plan for carrying the Water direct into the Black-a-Brook & requested it might be conveyed under their Leat by a Tunnel of sufficient strength'.[140]

Not to be thwarted, Tyrwhitt entered into negotiations with PDWC himself,

A line of rushes marks the route of the foul leat on Royal Hill.
Elisabeth Stanbrook.

85

which held up proceedings somewhat. In mid-August the Board informed him that if his leat was not completed by 1 September, they would 'carry a Leat direct to the Blackabrook under the Plymouth Dock Water Company's Leat'.[141] Four days later Tyrwhitt was able to announce that he had now arranged with the water company for his leat to be dug.

The dry course of the foul leat can still be traced in part. It ran close to and parallel with the higher side of the Devonport Leat for about a mile, crossing under the Two Bridges road. It then continued through Tor Royal newtake, encircling Royal Hill, Broken Borough and Strane Head at approximately the 1,275 ft (c.385m) contour, though much of it is very indistinct. It is most evident north and south of the head of the Cholake where its course can be seen both as a line of rushes and as a dry leat channel. Its point of entry into the newtake appears to have been by means of an aqueduct carrying it over the Devonport Leat and low ground a few hundred metres south of Tor Royal House.

Both the clean and foul water channels gave cause for concern during the first few years. Not least was the weather - for example, in January 1809 frost and snow had frozen them solid. In February Mr Henry Rowe had been employed by the Board at a salary of £63 p.a. to superintend the water courses and, in early March, Mr Hemmingway announced they would be finished shortly.

A year later, in March 1810, the water courses were in such a bad condition that it was felt they needed to be made deeper and laid with larger stones which would prove to be very expensive especially as the prisoners found great difficulty working with moor stone. A letter expressing regret at the state of them was sent to Mr Alexander, and asking what should be done. His reply, from London Dock, said that the water courses were constructed to be adequate for their purposes and that they should be constantly looked at by a proper workman and that they should employ a navigator for this (his agent, Mr Hemmingway recommended Mr Peter Sermon). He suggested that Mr Isaac Telling, who constructed the works, should travel to Dartmoor Prison to undertake the repairs which would cost about £20. He also claimed that had these 'trifling damages' been repaired the water courses' poor condition could have been averted. Rising to this, Capt Cotgrave retorted that these 'trifling damages' were not repaired as they would have exceeded a workman's wages. By October, he had decided it was prudent to lower the clean water courses and have them covered.

In the meantime, the foul water leat was causing problems. It had become damaged and the repairs necessitated a trench to be cut to take away the foul water from the burying ground clear of the Devonport Leat!

APPENDIX II
Trouble at the Bakehouse

It would seem from the records that the bad quality of bread and the employment of informers (Messrs Fox, Bawden and Thorne) by the Board had serious consequences. Contractors supplying some of the flour to the bakehouse were Messrs Drake, Hagerman and Twynham. The consistently bad bread being supplied to the prison warranted investigation and the bakers, Mr Fox (who was a master miller) and Mr Bawden together with Mr Thorne, were employed by the Board to investigate the matter.

In 1813 Mr Fox took samples from some of the sacks of flour belonging to the contractors as they arrived at Dartmoor Prison. He made holes in each sack with a penknife and took about 4 ozs 'flour' from each and sent them to the Board. Examination of these samples showed that 52 sacks contained contaminated flour; it had been mixed with china clay and 'other Deleterious Articles by which many of the Prisoners died from 16 to 25 daily'.[142] It was at this time that the Mayor of Plymouth also discovered that local millers were selling flour impregnated with china clay; hundreds of tons had been bought from St Austell 'and used to adulterate even the Peninsula supplies'.[143]

Drake, Hagerman and Twynham were brought to trial and convicted at Exeter in 1814. But, somehow, Hagerman and Twynham escaped to France. Twynham enjoyed a contraband trade with England, having accumulated over £70,000 here. In 1815 Mr Thorne was anxious to go to Bordeaux in France to bring both men back to receive the sentence that awaited them. Hagerman then fled to Germany.

All three informers lived to regret their part in unveiling the contractors' misdemeanours. Poor Mr Fox was, for some reason, apprehended after his sample-taking exercise, charged with felony, and taken before Mr Morgan, the magistrate in Tavistock, where he was granted bail. He went before the Michaelmas Sessions for Devon in 1813 when the prosecutors got ten witnesses to appear against him. Fortunately, the Bill was thrown out; the judge presumably realised he had been framed. But the prosecution cost Mr Fox £4 10s and his living, 'the whole of the Trade being so connected refuses to give him labour'.[144] Having parted with every article of value he owned, he then appealed to the Lord Commissioners for money for flour to keep him and his wife and family out of the Poor House. On 25 April 1819, the Treasury ordered the Transport Board to pay him and Mr Bawden £10, and Mr Thorne £30. Thomson claims that, eventually, the Admiralty gave Mr Fox employment. Not having found any evidence for this, it can only be hoped that they did.

Mr Bawden was discharged from the bakehouse in August 1813. He 'was bred up a Labourer, in the Farming Line'[145] and employed as a labourer in the storeroom of the contractor's bakehouse. He went to live with Mr Thorne at his farm near Tavistock and stayed from harvest to winter until Mr Thorne was turned out and the farm shut up. His wife and six children continued to live near the prison in a cottage during this time and he brought out a week's wage to her.

Mr Thorne, who had been a respectable master miller and farmer, became bankrupt. At the time of the trial he had a lawsuit with the Duke of Bedford about a farm, which completed his ruin. However, his troubles became known by Gill & Hornbrook who offered to employ him if the Board would give him a good reference. Strangely, Thomson claims that in 1814 Thorne gave evidence against Gill & Hornbrook on behalf of the Board. Had this been the case, it seems unlikely that they would have wanted to employ him.

APPENDIX III
The 1815 Massacre[146]

Report of Occurrence on 6 April 1815

'...a very alarming Riot broke out among the American Prisoners of War', wrote Mr J.H. Croker to the Lord Commissioners of the Admiralty concerning the incident at Dartmoor Prison, often referred to as the 'Princetown Massacre'.

The prisoners 'endeavoured to overpower the Guard to force the Prison and had actually seized the Arms of some of the Soldiery, and make a Breach in the Walls of the Depot, when the Guard found itself obliged to have recourse to their fire Arms and five of the Rioters were felled, and thirty four wounded'. The prisoners then calmed down to a state of 'tranquillity and security'.

John Duckworth, Commander-in-Chief, arrived from Plymouth and directed Rear Admiral Sir Josias Rowley Bart, CB, and Captain Schonberg, the two Plymouth Prison Officers, to proceed to Dartmoor and start an enquiry into the circumstances.

Dartmoor Prison Officers and the American prisoners were questioned. No cause was given for the conduct of the prisoners but they did express impatience for their release and blamed the American government for not sending 'means for their early conveyance home.'

Report of the English and American Commissioners

Dated 26 April 1815, the verdict on the prisoners deaths in this report was given as 'justifiable homicide'. There were eighty people attending the examination of witnesses, and many statements were contradictory. Up until the event itself the prisoners' frustrations at the slowness of their release were not expressed in violence although there had been threats to break out. On 2 April a large body of prisoners had rushed into the out-of-bounds market square and demanded bread instead of biscuit. This demand was met and they returned to their own yards.

However, events took a nasty turn on 6 April. At 6pm, a hole was found in a Prison wall large enough for a man to pass through. Other holes were found to have been started nearby. Some of the prisoners had got over the railings, which was forbidden, and were tearing up turf and throwing it at each other in 'a noisy and disorderly manner'. More prisoners collected in the yard where the hole had been made. The horn had sounded for prisoners to return to their respective Prisons but they did not go which gave those in charge the cause for alarm.

The Guard Barrack in the yard in question was where arms were usually kept in racks. Although there was no evidence that the prisoners would take them, it was further cause for alarm.

Capt Shortland gave the order for the alarm bell to sound in order to collect together the military. It was felt this contributed towards what happened, although he was thought to be justified in his actions. The alarm bell resulted in many prisoners rushing out to see what was going on. Almost at the same instant the alarm bell was ringing, one or more prisoners broke the iron chain, which was the only fastening of No.1 Gate leading into the market square, by means of an iron bar. Many prisoners then rushed towards that gate. There was no evidence that this was planned or that prisoners had intended to escape, but Capt Shortland and the military assumed that the prisoners were on the point of breaking out; it would seem that the outer market gates had been opened to let in the bread wagon to go to the store.

Capt Shortland went to the square where the prisoners had gathered, having ordered about fifty guards to follow him. He and Dr Magrath then tried to persuade the prisoners to return to their own yards, 'explaining to them the fatal consequences which must ensue if they refused'. By this time, the military were two thirds of the way down the square and stretched the breadth of about 100 yards.

Although some prisoners did try to return, others pressed on, and so Capt Shortland ordered 'about 15 file of the Guard nearly in front of the Gate which had been forced, to charge the Prisoners back to their own Yards'. In the resulting struggle, some of the military showed reluctance, some prisoners tried to return and some pressed forward. But the charge was mostly

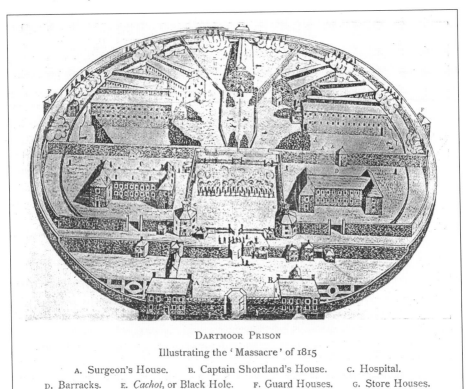

DARTMOOR PRISON

Illustrating the ' Massacre ' of 1815

A. Surgeon's House.   B. Captain Shortland's House.   C. Hospital.
D. Barracks.   E. *Cachot*, or Black Hole.   F. Guard Houses.   G. Store Houses.

An artist's impression of the 'Massacre of 1815'.

successful, leaving only a few prisoners by No.1 Gate. But a good crowd remained in the passage between the square and the Prison yards and yard gates. They refused to go and, according to English witnesses and some Americans, this crowd 'was making a noise, hallooing, insulting and provoking and daring the military to fire... and was pelting the military with large stones', some of which reached the target! However, other English and American witnesses denied this happened.

Then the firing started. Evidence as to whether the order was given was contradictory. Several Americans swore that Capt Shortland gave the order but their accounts differed so much that 'it is very difficult to reconcile this Testimony'. Many soldiers and English witnesses said they heard the word given by someone but could not swear it was Capt Shortland, or say who it was.

Capt Shortland denied that he had give the order to fire, and it was felt that it was improbable that he had. But whether the firing began in the square by order, or was a spontaneous act of the soldiers, 'It seemed clear, that it was continued, and ensued both there & elsewhere, without orders, and that on the platforms & in the Several places about the Prison, it was certainly commenced without any authority'.

The Commissioners felt that the firing 'was justifiable in a Military point of View, in order to intimidate the Prisoners and compel them thereby to disist from all Acts of Violence & to retire as they were ordered'.

As so few prisoners standing near the firing military were injured, it would appear, according to one or two witnesses, that most of the firing of muskets was levelled over the prisoners heads. This was partly lamented as it 'induced them to cry out "Blank Cartridge"' and continue their insults to the military. This resulted in a much more destructive nature of firing resulting in the injuries. The prisoners then started to run back to the prison, meaning the cause for the firing had ceased. The order came from Capt Shortland to stop firing.

So it was difficult to justify further firing in the Prison yards and elsewhere, although there was further provocation given to the military, resistance given to the turnkeys in shutting the prisons, and stones being thrown.

It seems subsequent firing arose from 'exasperation on the part of the soldiers, who followed the prisoners into the yards and from the absence of nearly all the Officers'. Capt Shortland was 'busily occupied by the Turnkeys in the Square, and caring and taking care of the wounded'. It was also the Officers' dinner time so fewer were on duty!

A cross fire was also going on at the same time as firing in the square from several platforms around the prison. The firing was successful in dispersing men from around the hole in the wall. But the Commissioners felt that firing on those prisoners returning to the prison seems to have been 'wholly without object or excuse, and to have been a wanton attack upon the lives of defenceless and at that time unoffending individuals'.

It was also proved that the firing took place in doorways to the Prisons, especially No.3, at a time when the men were crowded in the entrance, and bullet marks were found in the walls. 'This firing must have proceeded from Soldiers a very few feet from the doorway'. The fact that the prisoners were throwing insults and preventing turnkeys from closing doors, was no excuse.

Attempts were made to identify guilty soldiers and identifying a death with a particular soldier, but without success.

The report was signed by Commissioners Charles King and and Francis Seymour Larpent.

*List of American Prisoners Killed[147]

John Haywood from Virginia: 'the ball entered a little posterior to the acromion of the left shoulder, and passed obliquely upwards; made about the middle of the right side its egress of the neck'.

Thomas Jackson from New York: 'the ball entered the left side of the belly nearly in a line with the navel, and made its egress a little below the false ribs in the opposite side; a large portion of the intestinal canal protruded through the wound made by the ingress of the ball. He languished until 3 o'clock of the 7th, when he died'.

John Washington from Maryland: 'the ball entered at the squamore process of the left temporal bone, and passing through the head, made its exit a little below the cruceal ridge of the occipital bone'.

James Mann from Boston: 'the ball entered at the inferior angle of the left scapula, and lodged under the integument of the right pectoral muscle. In its course, it passed through the inferior margin of the right and left lobes of the lungs'.

Joseph Toker Johnson (from Connecticut): 'the ball entered at the inferior angle of the left scapula, penetrated the heart, and passing through both lobes of the lungs, made its egress at the right axilla'.

William Leverage from New York: 'the ball entered about the middle of the left arm, through which it passed, and penetrating the corresponding side, betwixt the second and third ribs, passing through the left lobe of the lungs, the mediartenum, and over the right lobe, lodged betwixt the fifth and sixth ribs'.

James Campbell from New York: 'the ball entered at the outer angle of the right eye, and in its course fractured and depressed the greater part of the frontal bone, fractured the nasal bones, and made its egress above the orbital ridge of the left eye. He languished until the morning of the 8th, when he died'.

*Names vary slightly according to different authors.

Appendix IV
Names Associated with Dartmoor Prison and Princetown
(excluding Militia and Prisoners)

George Abbot - licensee of Plume of Feathers

Mr Adams - surveyor of building work

Mr Adams (Transport Board)

John Alger - mason

Mr Daniel Asher Alexander - architect

John Arnold - turnkey/Hospital steward/receiver of letters

Richard Arnold - turnkey

Dr Baird - Transport Board Doctor

Samuel Barrett - turnkey

Mr Bawden - miller

Mr Reuben Beasley - American Agent

William Bell - Hospital mate

Mr Bennett - Agent for Tavistock

John Bennett - extra clerk/store clerk

W. Bennett - extra clerk

Mr Bennett - renter of Princetown brewery/miller

Thomas Bennett - yeoman

Samuel Best - turnkey

Mr Bicknell - solicitor

John Billing (Plymouth) - supplier of straw and birch brooms

T. Billing - victualler

Johnathan Birch - victualling sick prisoners

Mr Birt - n/k

M.A. Bobourg - assistant accountant

Mr Bond - carrier from Plymouth

William Bough - peat cutter

Jacob Bricknell - baker

Messrs Brock & Co - supplier of wine

James Broderick - timber supplier

Mary Brooke - seamstress

George Bryant (London) - supplier of lead

John Buckingham - first clerk

Revd Cape - instructor of R.E. to prisoners

James Carley - turnkey/Cachot keeper

Mr Carpenter - renter of slaughterhouse

Mr Edward Carter - occupier of a 'hut' - (labourer)

Cauldery & Son - lighter of lamps

George Challacombe - waggoner & labourer

Mrs Chapman - wife of Thomas

Thomas Chapman - canal man [ie leat man] & occupier of 'hut'

Mr W. Chonine - would-be purchaser of iron railway

Sam Coates - turnkey

Mrs Coates - wife of Sam

Mr William Cock - victualler

P. Coleman - prison employee

William Collard - baker

Anthony Cooper - occupier of a hut

James Cooper, bakehouse owner

Revd Coppin - instructor of R.E. to prisoners

Thomas Cowling - canal man [ie. leat man]

Richard Criper - licensee of Plume of Feathers

Sarah Criper - licensee of Plume of Feathers

John Crispin - turnkey

George Currie - Hospital mate/assistant surgeon

Thomas Davey - baker

Thomas Denty - labourer

R. Dick - Hospital mate

William Dickson - assistant surgeon

William Dovey - dispenser

Mr Drake - supplier of bread

John Duncan - Hospital turnkey

John Dunning - butcher at slaughterhouse

Thomas Dyer - Hospital steward

Mr William Dyker - surgeon

Nicholas Eales - carpenter

George Edgecombe - turnkey

Richard Edwards - baker

John Ellis - licensee of Duchy Hotel

Mary Ellis (Tavistock) - market trader

Robert Evely - labourer

William Falls - Hospital mate

Richard Fillis - renter of bakehouse/victualler

Mr Flaxman - unsuccessful applicant

Mr Fox - master miller

John French - turnkey

Messrs Gill & Co - suppliers, various

Gill & Hornbrook - Tavistock bakers

Frederick Gottelieb - turnkey

William Gray - acting surgeon

Messrs Hadley & Simpson (London) -
supplier of fire engine

Mr Hagerman - supplier of biscuits and flour

John Halfyard - master blacksmith

Richard Hall - provider of moor stone and
licensee of Rundlestone Inn

Stephen Hall - turnkey

Richard Hamden - turnkey

William Hammett - n/k

John Hannaford - turnpike keeper (in 1816)

Mr Hapham (Exeter) - provider of lamp
glasses

Robert Hardy - dispenser

Mr Hearle - store clerk

Mr Hemmingway - agent to Mr Alexander

Hugh Hill - labourer & recapturer of prisoner
F. Paulin

Messrs Hoine & Stackhouse (Liverpool) -
supplier of sheet lead

Elizabeth Holmden - assistant seamstress

R. Holmden - store clerk

Mr Howard - turnkey

Mr Hullet - farmer

T. Husband - supplier of lead

Mr Hutton - contractor for Hospital/renter of
slaughterhouse

William Huxham - supplier of goods

Messrs Isbell, Hartland, Rowe & Holland -
prison builders and victuallers of workmen

John Jeffrey - stone mason

Thomas Jennings - labourer

Peter Jermon - canal man [ie leat
man]/labourer]

Arthur Jewell - turnkey

Stephen Jewell - husbandman

Thomas Luckey Jewell - husbandman

Messrs Joliffe & Banks - suppliers of cement

Preacher Jones - from Plymouth

Richard Jones - Foreman of the Masons

William Jordan - shoemaker

John Kirton - sexton

J. Knapman - canteen clerk

Messrs Knight & Jones - suppliers

John Kroger - victualler

John Lakeman - licensee of Duchy Hotel

Mr Lane - surgeon

Robert Lane - landlord of Plume of Feathers

Messrs Langham & Harris - suppliers

Samuel Lawrence - labourer

Messrs Lindsay & Co - Prison victuallers

Messrs Lodge & Co - packers of bedding for
prison

Joseph Longman - part owner Mill Hill Slate
Quarry, Tavistock

John Lowday - licensee Plume of Feathers

Thomas Luckraft - baker

Dr George Magrath - surgeon

Mr McMann - n/k

James Cleave Madge - turnkey

Mr Magan - baker

Messrs Mann & Harrison (London) -
suppliers

Mr Marks - dispenser

John Martin (Tavistock) - prospective coffin supplier

Revd James Holman Mason - vicar of Dartmoor Church

William May - slater/mason

Martin Maynard - turnkey

John Middleton - labourer

John Miles - supplier of coverlets

John Mitchell - market/Hospital clerk

Jacob Monk - baker

John Moore - clerk & interpreter

John Morgan - turnkey

Samuel Morgan - turnkey

Mount Foundry Iron Co (Tavistock) - supplier of goods

John Newcombe - Hospital steward

Mr Newman - supplier of oil

David Nichols - turnkey

Messrs Noble & Hunt - suppliers

Mr Norman - lessee of land near church

William Norris - turnkey

Mr Nosworthy - supplier of timber

William Osmond - miller

Mr Parke - n/k

Mr Payne (Plymouth) - supplier of oil

Mr Payne - contractor of wine

Edmund Pearse - senior Hospital mate/ interpreter

William Pearse (Plymouth) - supplier of candles

Mr Pelling - supplier of timber

Tristram Physick - turnkey

David Pilmore - turnkey

John Pilmore - turnkey

Nathan G. Poulden - acting surgeon

John Price - labourer

Joseph Price - supplier of hammocks

William Reep (Nattor Farm) - supplier of dairy produce to Prison Hospital

Mr Roberts - labourer

John Rodd - turnkey

Robert Roddon - labourer at Princetown brewery

Thomas Rogers - investigator of poor bread

Henry Rowe - plumber, glazier and superintendent of water courses

James Rowe - master blacksmith

Joshua Rowe (Torpoint) - contractor/victualler

Mary Rowe - part owner Mill Hill Slate Quarry, Tavistock

Mr Sarman - occupier of a 'hut' - (labourer?)

William Scott - carpenter

Peter Sermon - navigator (water courses)

John Sharman - victualler

William Shillabeer - surveyor of prison lands

Charles Shipley - lamplighter

Thomas Skinner - baker

John Smith & Son - supplier of sacking for beds

William Smith - victualler

John Spray - Hospital mate

Messrs Start & Co - suppliers of elm board

William Stocker - licensee of Duchy Hotel

John Sweet (Plymouth) - Sheriff Officer

Mrs Tanzean - assistant seamstress

John Tapson - labourer

Isaac Telling - constructor of water courses

Martin Thomas - baker

Mr Thorne - renter of bakehouse

John Tozer - tailor/turnkey

William Treble - turnkey

Mr Trotter - storekeeper general

Mr Twynham - contractor of bread and flour

Mr (later Sir) Thomas Tyrwhitt

Robert Uren - moor stone mason

John Veitch - supplier of plants

Edward Vosper - mason

Mark Wakeham - turnkey

John Walters - architect and Foreman of the Works

William Warnale[?] - interpreter

Messrs Watkins & Brown - Hospital
  victuallers
John Watts - farmer and stone waller/turf
  supplier
Mr J. Webber - n/k
William Wells - supplier of goods
William Whiteway - turnkey/lessee of land
  near church
John Whithair - n/k
William Winch - licensee of Plume of
  Feathers
W.G. Winkworth - dispenser
Mr Winn - occupier of a 'hut' - labourer?
Mr Winnie - craftsman
Henry Winson - licensee of Duchy Hotel
Edward Worth - licensee of Duchy Hotel

REFERENCES

DCO(L) = Duchy of Cornwall Office (London); DRO = Devon Record Office; PWDRO = Plymouth & West Devon Record Office; PRO = Public Record Office; RCHME = Royal Commission on the Historical Monuments of England; WCSL = West Country Studies Library.

1. Catel, Louis (1847) *La Prison de Dartmoor* 2 Vols pp.5-6.
2. Andrews, Charles (1815) *The Prisoners Memoirs; or Dartmoor Prison* Privately published p.19.
3. PRO/ADM99/162 26.6.1805.
4. House of Commons Parliamentary Papers 1818 Vol.VIII p.178.
5. Brodie, A., Croom, J., & Davies, James O. (2002) *English Prisons - An Architectural History* English Heritage p.53.
6. Parliamentary Papers p.178.
7. PRO/ADM99/164 16.1.1806.
8. Thomson, Basil (1907) *The Story of Dartmoor Prison* William Heinemann pp.4-5.
9. Parliamentary Papers p.183.
10. An Act for Repairing the Road from Roborough Rock to the Tavistock Road near Dartmoor Prison of War and to Two Bridges, in the County of Devon. 28 February 1812.
11. Thomson, B. p.8.
12. PRO/ADM99/166 16.4.1806.
13. PRO/ADM99/169 26.7.1806.
14. PRO/ADM99/181 20.10.1807.
15. PRO/ADM99/193 28.12.1808.
16. ibid. 20.12.1808.
17. ibid 29.10.1808.
18. PRO/ADM99/194 24.11.1808.
19. PRO/ADM99/193 19.12.1808.
20. ibid. 20.12.1808.
21. loc. cit.
22. ibid. 19.11.1808.
23. PRO/ADM98/225 19.10.1808.
24. Parliamentary Papers p.173.
25. PRO/ADM99/195 29.1.1809.
26. PRO/ADM98/225 29.4.1809.
27. ibid. 23.5.1809.
28. Whitfield, H. (1900) *Plymouth and Devonport in Times of War and Peace* Hiorns & Miller p.245.
29. Hemery, Eric (1983) *High Dartmoor* Robert Hale Ltd p.178.
30. Catel, L. p.6.
31. Parliamentary Papers p.179.

32. H.M. Prison Dartmoor Report (n.d.) RCHME p.15.
33. Parliamentary Papers p. 172 & 175.
34. Photocopy of Regulations supplied by Michael Chamberlain.
35. Thomson, B. p.45.
36. Parliamentary Papers p.195.
37. Andrews, C. pp.40-1.
38. Catel. L. pp.171-7.
39. PRO/ADM98/225 27.12.1809.
40. H.M. Prison Dartmoor Report pp.15-16.
41. PRO/ADM98/225 29.11.1809.
42. Parliamentary Papers p.187.
43. loc. cit.
44. ibid. p.179
45. ibid. p.173
46. Abell, Francis (1914) *Prisoners of War in Britain 1756-1815* Oxford University Press p.241.
47. Parliamentary Papers p.177.
48. ibid. p.176.
49. ibid. p.175
50. ibid. p.176.
51. PRO/ADM99/203 3.5.1810.
52. Regulations photocopy.
53. PRO/ADM99/202 27.3.1810.
54. Thomson, B. pp.26-7.
55. PRO/ADM99/202 4.4.1810.
56. Catel, L. p.21.
57. PRO/ADM98/225 24.12.1810.
58. Parliamentary Papers p.180.
59. ibid. p.172.
60. Regulations photocopy.
61. Crossing, William (1989) *Princetown - Its Rise & Progress* Quay Publications (Brixham) p.36 and Fox, Sheila 'Princetown'. Transcript of an article in *Tavistock Times* 19.5.1965.
62. PRO/ADM99/201 26.2.1810.
63. ibid. 6.1.1810.
64. PRO/ADM99/207 26.6.1811.
65. PRO/ADM98/226 27.8.1811.
66. PRO/ADM98/226 20.5.1811.
67. ibid. 21.11.1811.
68. H.M. Prison Dartmoor Report p.15.
69. PRO/ADM99/217 23.8.1812.
70. PRO/ADM99/220 1.9.1812.

71. PRO/ADM98/306 29.2.1812.
72. PRO/ADM99/219 19.9.1812.
73. PRO/ADM98/306 21.9.1812.
74. PRO/ADM99/220 26.10.1812.
75. PRO/ADM99/223 27.11.1812.
76. Parliamentary Papers p.179.
77. Stanbrook, Elisabeth (1994) *Dartmoor Forest Farms - A Social History from Enclosure to Abandonment* Devon Books p.68.
78. Personal communication with Ron Joy, 2002.
79. PRO/ADM98/227 7.11.1812.
80. Andrews, C. p.22.
81. PRO/ADM99/241 21.8.1813.
82. PRO/ADM99/247 18.11.1813.
83. Parliamentary Papers p.196.
84. Lowe, M.C. (1998) 'Devon Local Carriers' in *Transactions of the Devonshire Association* p.116.
85. Jones, Revd J.P. (1823) *Observations on the Scenery and Antiquities in the Neighbourhood of Moretonhampstead and on the Forest of Dartmoor* R. Bond p.47.
86. ibid. p.48.
87. Andrews, C. p.64.
88. PRO/ADM99/251 18.1.1814.
89. PRO/ADM99/253 26.2.1814.
90. loc. cit.
91. PRO/ADM98/228 16.5.1814.
92. ibid. 11.3.1814.
93. ibid. 22.9.1814.
94. ibid. 7.11.1814.
95. Velpey, Joseph (1922) *Journal of Joseph Velpey, Jr of Salem November 1813 - April 1815* Michigan Society of Colonial Wars pp.13-14.
96. ibid. p.25.
97. PRO/ADM98/228 10.11.1814.
98. Parliamentary Papers p.202.
99. PRO/ADM98/228 16.5.1814.
100. ibid. 8.6.1814.
101. Velpey, J. p.13.
102. Parliamentary Papers p.181.
103. PRO/ADM98/228 6.7.1814.
104. Velpey, J. p.18.
105. ibid. p.16.
106. ibid. p.20.
107. ibid. p.26.

108. PRO/ADM98/228 2.6.1815.
109. ibid. 20.7.1815.
110. Parliamentary Papers p.186.
111. PRO/ADM98/228 29.7.1815.
112. PRO/ADM98.229 15.8.1815.
113. ibid. 12.12.1815.
114. ibid. 2.2.1816.
115. ibid. 8.1.1817.
116. Parliamentary Papers p.178.
117. DCO(L) Enclosure Bill Book 1797.
118. DRO/564 Swete, John (1797) 'Picturesque Sketches of Devon' Vol.16 p.151.
119. WCSL Ordnance Surveyors Drawings 1802-3.
120. DRO/S64 op. cit.
121. *The Bristol Times & Mirror* 15.7.1805.
122. PRO/ADM99/213 14.12.1811.
123. PRO/ADM98/227 10.1.1812.
124. Personal communication with The Church of England Record Centre 21.3.02.
125. PRO/ADM98/227 10.1.1812.
126. loc. cit.
127. PRO/ADM99/213 30.1.1812.
128. PRO/ADM99/222 1.11.1812.
129. PRO CRES 2/199.
130. Burt, W. (1826) 'Notes to Dartmoor' in Carrington, N.T. *Dartmoor: A Descriptive Poem* Hatchard & Son.
131. PRO/ADM99/250 8.1.1814 & 13.1.1814.
132. PRO/ADM98/228 25.5.1814.
133. Andrews, C. p.90.
134. Harris, Capt Vernon (c.1875) *Dartmoor Prison Past and Present* Brendon & Son p.28.
135. PRO/ADM98/228 13.8.1814.
136. ibid. 26.12.1814.
137. PWDRO Princetown Burial Register.
138. PRO/ADM98/229 12.12.1815.
139. PRO/ADM99/187 11.5.1808.
140. PRO/ADM99/188 13.6.1808.
141. PRO/ADM99/189 17.8.1808.
142. PRO/ADM105/60 16.6.1819.
143. Whitfield, H. p.238.
144. PRO/ADM105/60 16.6.1819.
145. ibid.
146. PRO/FO951/2 10.4.1815 & 26.4.1815.
147. Andrews, C. pp.184-5.

ACKNOWLEDGEMENTS

I am indebted to the following libraries and record offices for their invaluable help in compiling this book: Devon Record Office, Plymouth & West Devon Record Office, West Country Studies Library, Duchy of Cornwall (London), Public Record Office, British Library, Church of England Record Centre, The Churches Conservation Trust, Hampshire County Council Museums Service and Oxford University Press.

Crown copyright material is reproduced by permission of English Heritage acting under licence from the Controller of Her Majesty's Stationery Office.

I would also like to thank the following people for their generous help and support: Maureen Attrill (Plymouth City Museum and Art Gallery), Michael Chamberlain, Bob and Gibby Edson, Tom Greeves, Pauline and Peter Hamilton-Leggett, Trevor James, Graham Johnson (Governor H.M. Prison Dartmoor) Ron Joy, Keith Mckay (Dartmoor National Park Authority) and Stephen Woods.

The quotations from Perez Drinkwater's letters appear by kind permission of Bruce Felknor (www.usmm.org) and Kimberley A. Van Derveer who is a direct descendant.

Although revised and with additions, much of the chapter on Princetown Church was first published in the *Transactions of the Devonshire Association* 1996, and I am grateful to the Editor for his kind permission to reproduce it here.

BIBLIOGRAPHY

Abell, Francis (1914) *Prisoners of War in Britain 1756-1815* Oxford University Press

Andrews, C. (1815) *The Prisoner's Memoirs; or Dartmoor Prison* Privately Printed

Atholl, J. (1953) *Prison on the Moor: the Story of Dartmoor Prison* John Long Ltd

Brodie, A., Croom, J., & Davies, James O. (2002) *English Prisons - An Architectural History* English Heritage

Burt, W., 1826. Notes to Dartmoor, in Carrington, N. T. *Dartmoor: A Descriptive Poem* (Hatchard & Son, London).

Carrington, N.T. (1826) *Dartmoor: A Descriptive Poem* Hatchard & Son

Catel, L (1847) *La Prison de Dartmoor*

Cherry, B. & Pevsner, N., 1989. *The Buildings of England: Devon* (Penguin Books, London).

Crossing, W. (1967) *A Hundred Years on Dartmoor* David & Charles

Crossing, W. (1965) *Guide to Dartmoor* David & Charles

Crossing, W. (1966) *Crossing's Dartmoor Worker* David & Charles

Crossing, W. (1989) *Princetown - Its Rise and Progress* Quay Publications (Brixham)

Gill C. (ed) (1970) *Dartmoor: A New Study* David & Charles

Gregg, Pauline (1977 edn) *A Social and Economic History of Britain 1760-1972* George G. Harrup & Co Ltd

Harris, Capt Vernon (c1875) *Dartmoor Prison, Past and Present* Brendon & Son

Hemery, E. (1983) *High Dartmoor - Land and People* Robert Hale Ltd

Hill, H.S. (1869) *Prince Town: Its History and its Prison* Latimer

Hoskins, W.G. (1966) *Old Devon* David & Charles

James, Trevor (1999) 'Sir Thomas Tyrwhitt - A Brief Appraisal' in *Dartmoor Magazine* 54

Jones, Rev J.P. (1823) *Observations on the Scenery and Antiquities in the Neighbourhood of Moretonhampstead and on the Forest of Dartmoor* R. Bond

Lowe, M.C. (1998) 'Devon Local Carriers' in *Transactions of the Devonshire Association* Devonshire Association

Niles Weekly Register (8 July 1815) 'Dartmoor Massacre'

Palmer, B.F. (1914) *Diary of Benjamin F. Palmer*

Parish Registers: Lydford and Princetown

Pierce, N. (c.1815) *Journal of Nathaniel Pierce 1814-1815*

Richardson, A.E. & Gill, C.L. (1924) *Regional Architecture of the West of England* Ernest Benn

Stanbrook, E. (1996) 'The Building of Princetown Church, Dartmoor: A Unique Monument to French and American Prisoners of War' *Rep. Transactions of the Devonshire Association.*

Stanbrook, E. (1994) *Dartmoor Forest Farms - A Social History from Enclosure to Abandonment* Devon Books

Thomson, Sir B. (1907) *The Story of Dartmoor Prison* Heinemann

Velpey, Joseph (1922) *Journal of Joseph Velpey, Jr of Salem November 1813 - April 1815* Michigan Society of Colonial Wars

Vancouver, Charles (1808) *General View of the Agriculture of the County of Devon*

White, William, 1850. *History, Gazetteer and Directory of Devonshire* (David & Charles, Newton Abbot)

Whitfield, H. (1900) *Plymouth & Devonport in Times of War and Peace* Hiorns & Miller

Woollcombe, Rev L.A.W. (1926) *Princetown and its Prison* Privately Printed

Worth, R. Hansford, 1941. 'Dartmoor 1788-1808' *Rep. Transactions of the Devonshire Association.*, 73, 203-25

INDEX